Wisdom of the Analects

Translated by Shen Fei
Academic Adviser: Zhang Baoquan
Compiled by Yu Jingsong
Proofread by Zhang Baoquan
Illustrated by Lan Xuehui   Zheng Zhenming
Cover Designed by Sarah Ma

Original of this edition: © Copyright 2016 Guangxi Normal University Press

English edition
Design Media Publishing (UK) Limited
http://www.designmediauk.com
E-mail: info@designmediauk.com
ISBN: 978-1-83865-001-8

© Copyright 2019 Design Media Publishing (UK) Limited

Printed in China

All rights reserved. The partial or total reproduction of this work by printing, reprography, microfilm, computer processing or any other means is prohibited without written authorisation from the publisher.

Any form of reproduction, distribution, public communication or similar processing of this work should only be carried out with the express permission of the publisher unless otherwise specified by law.

Wisdom of the Analects

DESIGN MEDIA

Preface to the Wisdom of the East Series

Cultural exchanges are of significant importance to the existence and development of human society. Mr. Ji Xianlin once pointed out that cultural exchange was one of the major driving forces for the progress of human society. It is inevitable that communications and exchanges will occur among different cultures. As a result, the interaction and mutual enrichment of cultures contribute to the formation of a diversified world featured by cultural prosperity.[1]

The cultural exchange between China and ASEAN countries, in the trend of mutual communication and interaction, also boasts of its own unique strengths. First of all, China borders many ASEAN countries both by land and by sea, and intermarriage and transnational settlement are common, all of which lay a solid foundation for cultural exchanges. In addition, the "Maritime Silk

---

[1] Ji Xianlin, "Preface to Cultural Conflicts and Integration", in *Cultural Conflicts and Integration*, edited by Zhang Dainian, Tang Yijie, et al. Beijing: Beijing University Press, 1997, p.2.

Road" developed by ancient China and other countries has helped pave the way to a smooth economic and cultural exchange between China and ASEAN countries.

People from China and ASEAN countries use different languages. Thus, to conduct a successful dialogue in the cultural field requires the involvement of translation and oral interpretation. Historical records show that the oral interpretation among people of China and ASEAN can be dated back to the Western Zhou Dynasty (1122-771 B.C.). It is also known that translation started to boom in the Ming Dynasty, which was five hundred years ago.

In the past five hundred years, a large number of Chinese cultural works were translated into many languages of ASEAN countries and many of which have been integrated into their local cultures. China has also translated a lot of works of ASEAN countries. Translation is beneficial to inheritance and development of culture and upgrades the cultural exchanges between China and ASEAN to a higher level.

As Mr. Li Keqiang, Premier of the State Council of the People's Republic of China, pointed out in his speech at the opening ceremony of the 10th China-ASEAN Expo held in Nanning in September, 2013, China and ASEAN jointly created "10 golden years" of cooperation. And he called on both sides to upgrade their cooperation to a new level by creating "10 diamond years". In October, 2013, General Secretary Xi Jinping emphasized, in a meeting with Chinese diplomats, the importance of introducing China's domestic and foreign policies to other countries and regions, and making Chinese voice heard in the world. Xi also pointed out that "Chinese Dream" should be connected with her neighboring countries' dream of a better life and with the development prospect of those countries so as to build up a community of shared destiny. Against such a backdrop, it's of both historical and current significance to translate Chinese classics and introduce them to ASEAN countries.

Exchanges are reciprocal. According to *The Book of Rites*, behaviors that do not reciprocate are not consistent with rites. Like ASEAN countries, China has had excellent foreign cultural works translated and introduced domestically, and also translate and introduce to the outside world the essence of local culture and thoughts. Guangxi Normal University Press, one of the top presses in China that focus on enhancing the influence of the humanities, made the decision to publish *The Wisdom of the East Series*. It is not only a big event in Chinese academia, but also a necessary choice for China and ASEAN to communicate with each other and enhance mutual understanding. Guangdong University of Foreign Studies, and Guangxi University for Nationalities, the main undertakers of the translation project, are both national non-universal languages training bases for undergraduates and boast strengths of ASEAN languages. Cooperation between the two universities and the press will surely facilitate dissemination of traditional Chinese culture to ASEAN countries.

UNESCO officials hold the belief that cultural exchange is a new phenomenon of globalization.[2] We hope that our efforts could breathe the spirit of this historical momentum and help ASEAN countries understand Chinese culture better.

Liu Zhiqiang
January 25, 2015

---

2 "Speech of Katerina stenou, Director of Division of Cultural Policies and Intercultural Dialogue", from *East Asia's View on World Culture*. Beijing: Beijing University Press, 2004, p.3.

总　序

　　文化交流对人类社会的存在与发展至关重要。季羡林先生曾指出，文化交流是推动人类社会前进的主要动力之一，文化一旦产生，就必然交流，这种交流是任何力量也阻挡不住的。由于文化交流，世界各民族的文化才能互相补充，共同发展，才能形成今天世界上万紫千红的文化繁荣现象。[1]

　　中国与东盟国家的文化交流亦然，并且具有得天独厚的优势。首先，中国与东盟许多国家地理相接，山水相连，不少民族之间普遍存在着跨居、通婚现象，这为文化交流奠定了良好的地理与人文基础。其次，古代中国与世界其他国家建立起的"海上丝绸之路"为中国与东盟国家的经济、文化交流创造了有利的交通条件。

　　中国与东盟诸多使用不同语言文字的民族进行思想与文化对话，

---

[1] 季羡林：《文化的冲突与融合·序》，载张岱年、汤一介等《文化的冲突与融合》，北京大学出版社，1997年，第2页。

自然离不开翻译。翻译活动一般又分为口译和笔译两类。有史记载的中国与东盟之间的口译活动可以追溯至西周时期，但笔译活动则出现在明代，至今已逾五百年的历史。

在过去五百年的历史长河中，东盟国家大量地译介了中国的文化作品，其中不少已经融入到本国的文化中去。中国译介东盟国家的作品也不在少数。以文字为载体的相互译介活动，更利于文化的传承与发展，把中国与东盟国家的文化交流推上了更高的层次。

2013年9月，国务院总理李克强在广西南宁举行的第十届中国—东盟博览会开幕式上发表主旨演讲时指出，中国与东盟携手开创了合作的"黄金十年"。他呼吁中国与东盟百尺竿头更进一步，创造新的"钻石十年"。2013年10月，习近平总书记在周边外交工作座谈会上强调要对外介绍好我国的内外方针政策，讲好中国故事，传播好中国声音，把中国梦同周边各国人民过上美好生活的愿望、同地区发展前景对接起来，让命运共同体意识在周边国家落地生根。于是，把中华文化的经典译介至东盟国家，不仅具有重要的历史意义，同时还蕴含着浓厚的时代气息。

所谓交流，自然包括"迎来送往"，《礼记》有言："往而不来，非礼也；来而不往，亦非礼也。"中国与东盟国家一样，既翻译和引进外国的优秀文化，同时也把本国文化的精髓部分推介出去。作为中国最具人文思想的出版社之一——广西师范大学出版社构想了《东方智慧丛书》，并付诸实践，不仅是中国翻译学界、人文学界的大事，更是中国与东盟进行良好沟通、增进相互了解的必然选择。广东外语外贸大学和广西民族大学作为翻译工作的主要承担方，都是国家外语非通用语种本科人才培养基地，拥有东盟语言文字的翻译优势。三个单位的合作将能够擦出更多的火花，向东盟国家更好地传播中华文化。

联合国教科文组织的官员认为："文化交流是新的全球化现象"。[2] 我们希望顺应这一历史潮流与时代趋势，做一点力所能及的事。

是为序。

刘志强
2015 年 1 月 25 日

---

[2]《联合国教科文组织文化政策与跨文化对话司司长卡特瑞娜·斯泰诺的致辞》，载《世界文化的东亚视角》，北京大学出版社，2004年，第3页。

孔子（公元前 551 年—公元前 479 年）
Confucius (551 BC - 479 BC)

Foreword

The *Analects* is a collection of sayings and ideas of Confucius, a great thinker and educator in ancient China and founder of Confucianism and his disciples. It's the most important classics for the Confucian school. Written by Confucius' disciples and his disciples of disciples at the early Warring States Period(476 BC-221 BC), the book covers the views of Confucius and the Confucian school on politics, ethics, morality and education.

Confucius is the kernel of the *Analects*. Confucius lived in the Spring and Autumn Period(770 BC-476 BC) of Chinese history, who was born on 28 September 551 BC in the State of Lu and died on 11 April 479 BC. Confucius' family name and personal name respectively was Kong and Qiu and his courtesy name was Zhongni. Confucius was one of the most learned persons of his time and was revered as Master Kong, the Sage Master and an "Exemplary Teacher for All Ages" by his later generations. Confucius was at the 1st place of UNESCO's list of world's top ten cultural celebrities. Most of the *Analects* records the ideas of Confucius and his behavior, manners and personality. And the book also displays distinct personalities of some of Confucius' disciples, like straightforward and rash Zilu, mild and studious Yan Hui, smart and eloquent Zigong, unrestrained and unconventional Zeng Xi, all leaving a deep impression on readers.

The *Analects* literally refers to a collection of sayings. The current version covers 20 books and the name of each book is the first two to three words of the first chapter of the book. As a collection of sayings, the *Analects* is compiled in a bit arbitrary way, yet each book has a relative concentration of themes and the books are logically connected to some degree.

The *Analects* covers politics, education, philosophy, literature and other aspects. It is divided generally into two parts: self-cultivation and the practice of government. Self-cultivation is concerned with being a person with the characteristics of humaneness, a high standard of morality, filial piety, respects for elder brothers, leniency, trustworthiness, honesty, generosity, studiousness, agility and many talents. A plethora of chapters of the *Analects* talk of the man of noble character. It's a general concept and stresses the pursuit of noble character and teaches people to be extraordinary persons. To help people achieve the goals, the *Analects* puts forward the behavior criteria and moral requirements of the man of noble character. For example, the man of noble character knows the value of righteousness while the mean man knows only the importance of gains and the man of noble character is slow in his words, but quick in his deeds(book of Li Ren) and the man of noble character seeks harmony rather than uniformity, while the mean man is the opposite (book of Zilu). Confucius paid great attention to education and taught his students tirelessly. He advocated individualized teaching and education for all without discrimination. With this in mind, Confucius broke the tradition of schools running by governments and started private teaching.

The practice of government in the *Analects* can be generalized into the following points: the foundation of running a country is that the ruler behaves like a ruler, the minister like a minister, the father like a father and the son like a son(book of Yan Yuan); Rulers should be self-disciplined and pay attention to credit. They should rule their countries with the power of morality and take care of their subjects. If a ruler behaves properly, how can it be difficult for him to rule his country? If not, how can he ask his subjects to be right in their doing? (book of Zilu). To rule a middle-sized state, the sovereign should be serious about his ruling over the state, keep his word and do not fool the common people, practice economy, properly use officials and use the common people to do public works in the slack season(book of Xue Er). The basic methods of running a country lie in selecting talented people, making the country prosper, cultivating people and making rules; Set a good example, forgive small mistakes and promote talented people. (book of Zilu) Ranyou asked, "If the country is populous, what should be done to the population?" The master said, "Enrich them." Ranyou asked, "When the population is rich, what else should be done to them?" The master said, "Educate them." (book of Zilu)

The *Analects* provides the firsthand information for the study of Confucius and Confucianism. The ideas, principles and theories established in the *Analects* exert far-reaching influence on its future generations. Zhao Pu, the politician in the Northern Song Dynasty (960 AD-1127 AD) said that the country can be well governed even by applying half of the *Analects*. Zhu Xi, a well-renowned scholar in the Southern Song Dynasty (1127 AD-1279 AD) recognized the *Analects* as one of the Four Books, together with the *Great Learning*, the *Doctrine of the Mean* and the *Works of Mencius*, greatly advancing its position in the classics of Confucianism. The *Analects* had been regarded as a classic by scholars until the end of the Qing Dynasty (1644 AD-1911 AD). The *Analects* remains as the most valuable historical and cultural classic of Chinese nation.

Thanks to the extensive influence of Confucius and Confucian ideas with the *Analects* as their core on the Korean peninsular, Japan and southeast Asia, the Confucian cultural circle was formed with China as its center. Currently, Confucianism is of an ever increasing importance to the world peace and development and the *Analects* should be known by more people.

The 100 sentences(chapters) in the book are the most quintessential of the *Analects*. They are accurately interpreted and painstakingly translated and matched with beautiful illustrations. It's proved itself to be a book of top quality for readers to understand Chinese Confucian culture.

前　言

　　《论语》是记载中国古代著名思想家、教育家、儒家学派创始人孔子及其弟子言行的语录体著作，是儒家学派最重要的经典，集中体现了孔子及儒家学派的政治主张、伦理思想、道德观念及教育原则等内容，成书于战国（公元前476年—前221年）初期，由孔子的弟子及其再传弟子记录而成。

　　孔子是《论语》的中心。孔子名丘，字仲尼，春秋时期（公元前770年—前476年）鲁国陬邑（今山东曲阜市南辛镇）人，生于公元前551年9月28日（农历八月二十七），卒于公元前479年4月11日（农历二月十一）。孔子集华夏上古文化之大成，是当时社会上最博学者之一，后世尊为孔圣人、至圣先师、万世师表，被联合国教科文组织评选为"世界十大文化名人"之首。《论语》大量篇章是直接体现孔子思想观点的语录，也有对孔子仪态举止、个性气质的传神描述。并且，围绕孔子这一中心，《论语》还成功地展现了一些孔门弟子的形象。如子路的率直鲁莽，颜回的温良好学，子贡的聪颖善辩，曾皙的潇洒脱俗等，都称得上个性鲜明，能给人留下深刻印象。

《论语》书名二字意为"言语汇编"，现通行本共二十篇，各篇皆以第一章正文（或语录）的前二三个字作为篇名。作为语录汇集，《论语》编纂有一定的随意性，但各篇有相对集中的主题，各篇之间也存在一定的逻辑性。

《论语》内容涉及政治、教育、哲学、文学等多方面，可简要概括为修身养德和治国安邦两大类。修身养德就是要做一个仁德、孝悌、恭谨、宽厚、信实、慈惠、勤敏、多才之人。《论语》许多篇幅谈及君子，君子是一个广义概念，重在强调一种人格追求，教人做一个不平凡的人。为实现这一目的，《论语》提出了君子的言行标准及道德修养要求。如："君子喻于义，小人喻于利"（《里仁》），"君子欲讷于言而敏于行"（《里仁》），"君子和而不同，小人同而不和"（《子路》），等等。孔子重视教育，诲人不倦，主张因材施教、有教无类，打破了学在官府的传统，开创私人讲学之风。

《论语》治国安邦思想可概括为以下几点：认为治国的根本在于建立"君君，臣臣，父父，子子"（《颜渊》）的人伦纲常；强调君主要严于律己，讲究信用，为政以德，爱护人民，"苟正其身矣，于从政乎何有？不能正其身，如正人何？"（《子路》），"道千乘之国，敬事而信，节用而爱人，使民以时"（《学而》）；治国的基本方法则是"选才、富国、育人、立法"，"先有司，赦小过，举贤才"（《子路》），"冉有曰：'既庶矣，又何加焉？'曰：'富之。'曰：'既富矣，又何加焉？'曰：'教之。'"（《子路》）

《论语》是研究孔子及儒家思想最重要的第一手资料，其所确立的观念、范畴、原则和理论，对后世影响极大。北宋（公元960年—1127年）政治家赵普曾有"半部《论语》治天下"之说。南宋（公元1127年—1279年）大儒朱熹将《大学》《中庸》《论语》《孟子》合为"四书",使之在儒家经典中的地位日益提高。直至清(公元1644年—1911年)末,《论语》一直被学子士人奉为经典。今天,《论语》依然是中华民族最可宝贵的历史文化典籍。

历史上,以《论语》为代表的孔子及儒家思想对朝鲜半岛、日本、东南亚等地区产生过深远影响,形成以中国为中心的儒家文化圈。当前,儒家思想对世界的和平与发展显现出越来越重要的意义,《论语》理应在更广的范围传播,奉献给世界人民。

本书精选《论语》最具代表性的100句(章),精确释析,精心翻译,并配绘精美插图,为了解中华儒家文化提供一个优质读本。

Contents

1. To learn and review from time to time what is learned 2
2. The man of noble character devotes himself to the fundamentals 4
3. I examine myself several times a day 8
4. Fulfill their filial duties at home and obey their elder brothers when away from home 10
5. Value virtues more than lust upon a young woman 12
6. Carefully attend to the funeral rites of one's parents and earnestly worship one's ancestors 16
7. Gentleness, kindness, courtesy, restraint and magnanimity 18
8. In the practice of rites, harmony is to be prized 22
9. The person is poor, but finds delight in pursuing knowledge, or rich, but observing the rites 24
10. Rule a country on the basis of morality 28
11. The general public is directed by moral education and constrained by rites 30
12. Establish myself at 30 and have no doubts about the world at 40 32
13. Derive new reflections from reviewing what one's learnt 36

目 录

1. 学而时习之 3
2. 君子务本 5
3. 吾日三省吾身 9
4. 入则孝，出则弟 11
5. 贤贤易色 13
6. 慎终追远 17
7. 温良恭俭让 19
8. 礼之用，和为贵 23
9. 贫而乐，富而好礼 25
10. 为政以德 29
11. 道之以德，齐之以礼 31
12. 三十而立，四十而不惑 33
13. 温故而知新 37

14. He who is steeped in learning but neglecting thinking feels perplexed while he who is absorbed in thinking but neglecting learning puts himself in danger 40
15. Say yes when you know and no when you don't, it's the wisdom 42
16. With fewer mistakes in your words and fewer regrets in your deeds, you can obtain a government position and receive an official's salary 46
17. An untrustworthy person cannot establish himself in the world 50
18. what is subtracted and added is knowable 52
19. How can a person with no humaneness observe rites 54
20. Being economical is better than extravagant at ritual ceremonies 58
21. The ruler should use his ministers in accordance with rites and his ministers should serve his ruler with loyalty 60
22. The man of noble character will never deviate from humaneness for even the time of a simple meal 64
23. If I know the Way in the morning, I can die without regrets at night ... 68
24. The man of noble character takes action in accordance with righteousness 70
25. One should worry not about obtaining no official positions, but about not qualified for that position 72
26. There is one main thread throughout my teaching 76
27. The man of noble character understands righteousness while the mean man knows only profits 78
28. When you see the man with virtues, try to emulate him 80
29. When waiting on parents, children should euphemistically persuade their parents into correcting their mistakes 84
30. Being slow to speak for fear of not suiting their deeds to their words 86
31. Self-disciplined people scarcely make any mistakes 88
32. Being slow to speak, but quick to act 92

14. 学而不思则罔，思而不学则殆 41

15. 知之为知之，不知为不知，是知也 43

16. 言寡尤，行寡悔，禄在其中矣 47

17. 人而无信，不知其可也 51

18. 损益可知 53

19. 人而不仁，如礼何 55

20. 礼，与其奢也，宁俭 59

21. 君使臣以礼，臣事君以忠 61

22. 君子无终食之间违仁 65

23. 朝闻道，夕死可矣 69

24. 义之与比 71

25. 不患无位，患所以立 73

26. 吾道一以贯之 77

27. 君子喻于义，小人喻于利 79

28. 见贤思齐 81

29. 事父母几谏 85

30. 言之不出，耻躬之不逮也 87

31. 以约失之者鲜矣 89

32. 讷于言而敏于行 93

33. Infer ten things from one he has learnt 94
34. Rotten wood cannot be carved 98
35. The elder are taken good care of and live in comfort, friends trust each other and the young have good examples to follow 102
36. Remain cheerful with only a small bamboo basket of rice to eat and a gourdful of water to drink 106
37. With perfect mix of simplicity and refinement, one can be called the man of noble character 108
38. Liking it is better than understanding it while enjoying it is the best ... 110
39. The wise love water while the humane love mountains 114
40. If you want to be established, help others be established. If you want to achieve success, help others achieve their success 116
41. Learn and never feel content. Teach tirelessly 120
42. Draw inferences about other cases from one instance 122
43. Follow my own inclinations 124
44. Wealth and rank achieved by improper means are like floating clouds 128
45. There is always someone for me to learn from 132
46. If I want to achieve it, the humaneness will be at hand 134
47. A scholar should be unyielding for he shoulders a heavy responsibility and has a long way to go 138
48. The *Book of Songs* inspires us 140
49. The master is free of the four defects 142
50. Inquire about both pros and cons of the question 146
51. The young deserve to be treated with awe 150
52. A man will not be deprived of his aspirations 152
53. It's not until the weather turns extremely cold can we see the leaves of pines and cypresses are the last to wither and fall 156

33. 闻一以知十 95

34. 朽木不可雕也 99

35. 老者安之，朋友信之，少者怀之 103

36. 箪食瓢饮不改其乐 107

37. 文质彬彬，然后君子 109

38. 知之者不如好之者，好之者不如乐之者 111

39. 知者乐水，仁者乐山 115

40. 己欲立而立人，己欲达而达人 117

41. 学而不厌，诲人不倦 121

42. 举一反三 123

43. 从吾所好 125

44. 不义而富且贵，于我如浮云 129

45. 三人行，必有我师焉 133

46. 我欲仁，斯仁至矣 135

47. 士不可以不弘毅，任重而道远 139

48. 兴于《诗》 141

49. 子绝四 143

50. 叩其两端 147

51. 后生可畏 151

52. 匹夫不可夺志 153

53. 岁寒，然后知松柏之后凋也 157

54. The wise have no puzzlement, the humane have no worries and the brave have no fears 158
55. Ask about casualty after the stable caught a fire 162
56. We have not yet known life, how can we know death? 166
57. Discipline yourself and act in accordance with rites. It's humaneness 168
58. All men under heaven are his brothers 172
59. If the common people are wanting in money, how can the sovereign have enough to spend? 176
60. The ruler should behave like a ruler, the minister like a minister, the father like a father, and the son like a son 178
61. The man of noble character helps others achieve their virtuous purposes 182
62. If you are an upright ruler, who else will not be upright? 184
63. If you are not greedy for money, you will not see burglars even though rewarding people for being burglars 188
64. The humane love others 190
65. Set a good example and forgive the small mistakes of others and promote people with talents and virtues 192
66. If the name is not correct, the words won't be justified 196
67. If the ruler acts properly, the common people will obey him without being ordered to 198
68. Educate people after they become rich 202
69. Speed hinders you from achieving goals 206
70. Seek harmony rather than uniformity 208
71. Fortitude, perseverance, artlessness and discreet are close to humaneness 210
72. He who is reluctant to give up his comfort family life is unworthy of a scholar 214
73. The man of noble character is ashamed of too much talk but not enough action 216

54. 知者不惑，仁者不忧，勇者不惧 **159**

55. 厩焚问人 **163**

56. 未知生，焉知死 **167**

57. 克己复礼为仁 **169**

58. 四海之内皆兄弟 **173**

59. 百姓不足，君孰与足 **177**

60. 君君，臣臣，父父，子子 **179**

61. 君子成人之美 **183**

62. 子帅以正，孰敢不正 **185**

63. 苟子之不欲，虽赏之不窃 **189**

64. 仁者爱人 **191**

65. 先有司，赦小过，举贤才 **193**

66. 名不正，则言不顺 **197**

67. 其身正，不令而行 **199**

68. 富而后教 **203**

69. 欲速则不达 **207**

70. 和而不同 **209**

71. 刚毅木讷，近仁 **211**

72. 士而怀居，不足以为士矣 **215**

73. 君子耻其言而过其行 **217**

74. Knowing it's of no use, but keeping on doing it 220
75. Cultivate yourself and make the common people live in happiness and peace 222
76. When in destitution, the man of noble character will preserve his moral integrity 226
77. Sacrifice his life for humaneness 230
78. A craftsman must sharpen his tools first if he is to do his work well ... 234
79. He who lacks long-term plans will have worries at hand 238
80. Reproach others less and question yourself more 240
81. Do not recommend a person because of his words. Do not ignore a person's good suggestions because of his deeds 242
82. Do not impose on others what you yourself do not desire 246
83. Lack of patience in small matters leads to the disruption of great plans 248
84. If one is hated by all, find out reasons 252
85. It's men who carry forward the Way 254
86. A mistake is a real mistake if not corrected 258
87. Students don't have to be inferior to their teachers concerning humaneness 260
88. Teach all with no discrimination 264
89. The trouble lies not in a small population but in uneven distribution of wealth, not in poverty but in instability 266
90. The man of noble character should always guard against three things 268
91. By nature, men are much alike; but in practice, they are far apart 272
92. He who likes humaneness but dislikes learning will be fooled 274
93. How can he with a full stomach but empty head achieve something? 276
94. The past cannot be retrieved, yet the future can be remedied 280

74. 知其不可而为之 221

75. 修己以安百姓 223

76. 君子固穷 227

77. 杀身成仁 231

78. 工欲善其事，必先利其器 235

79. 人无远虑，必有近忧 239

80. 躬自厚而薄责于人 241

81. 不以言举人，不以人废言 243

82. 己所不欲，勿施于人 247

83. 小不忍则乱大谋 249

84. 众恶之，必察焉 253

85. 人能弘道 255

86. 过而不改，是谓过矣 259

87. 当仁，不让于师 261

88. 有教无类 265

89. 不患寡而患不均，不患贫而患不安 267

90. 君子有三戒 269

91. 性相近也，习相远也 273

92. 好仁不好学，其蔽也愚 275

93. 饱食终日，无所用心，难矣哉 277

94. 往者不可谏，来者犹可追 281

95. Scholars sacrifice their lives in times of danger, keep righteousness in mind in front of profits 284
96. Learn extensively while sticking to one's interests, ask questions earnestly and give more thoughts to the current issues 286
97. A scholar, after completing his learning, should devote himself to duties as an official 290
98. Mistakes made by the man of noble character are like eclipses of the sun and the moon 294
99. Direct people to get what are beneficial to them 296
100. He who doesn't know his destiny will not be the man of noble character 298

95. 士见危致命，见得思义 285

96. 博学笃志，切问近思 287

97. 学而优则仕 291

98. 君子之过也，如日月之食焉 295

99. 因民之所利而利之 297

100. 不知命，无以为君子也 299

学而时习之

To learn and review from time to time what is learned

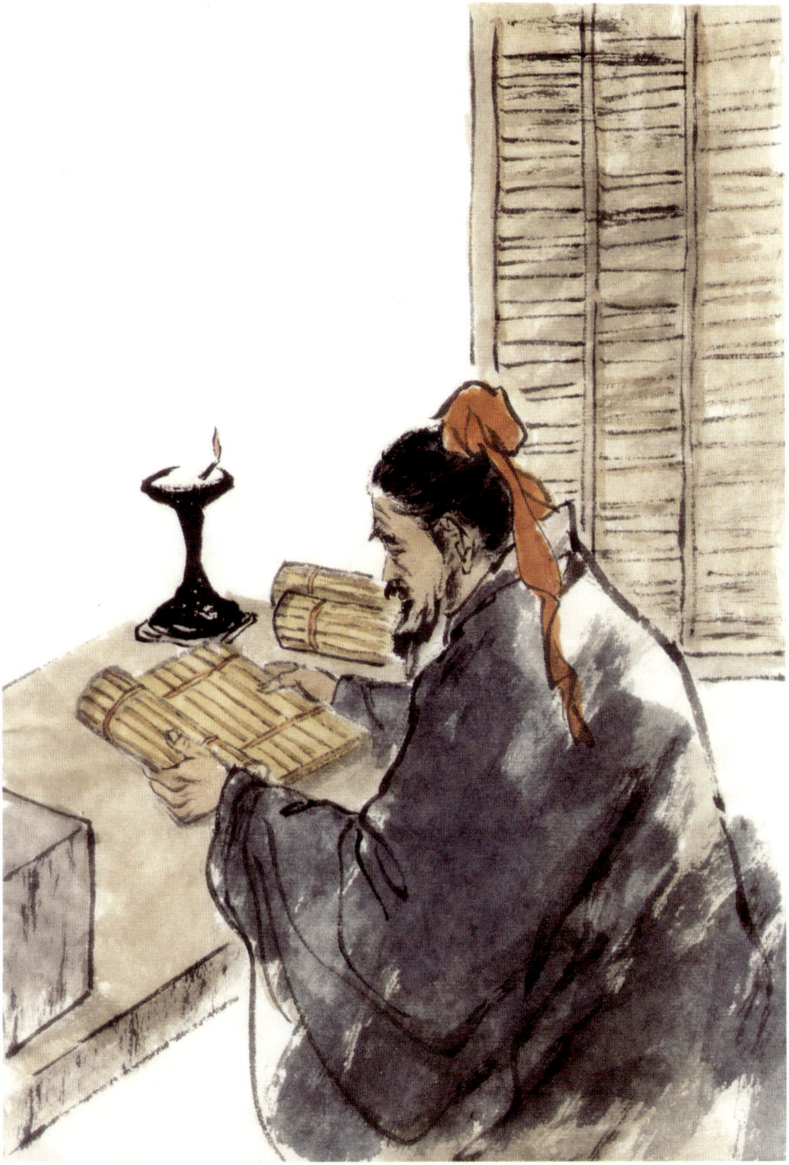

1. To learn and review from time to time what is learned

【Source】

　　The Master said, "Is it not a pleasure to learn and review from time to time what is learned? Is it not a delight to have friends coming from afar? Is it not the man of noble character who bears no grudges when not being recognized?"

The Analects· Xue Er Chapter1.1

【Comments】

　　The chapter emphasizes taking learning as a great pleasure and not feeling angry when not being recognized. It reflects the view of Confucius on having insatiable desire to learn, teaching tirelessly and focusing on self-cultivation and self-discipline.

1. 学而时习之

【原文】

子曰:"学而时习之,不亦说乎?有朋自远方来,不亦乐乎?人不知而不愠,不亦君子乎?"

《论语·学而》1.1 章

【释文】

孔子说:"学了又按时温习和练习,不是很愉快吗?有志同道合的人从远方来,不是很令人高兴吗?人家不了解我,我也不怨恨、恼怒,不也是一个有德的君子吗?"

【解析】

本章提出以学习为乐事,做到人不知而不愠,反映出孔子学而不厌、诲人不倦、注重修养、严格要求自己的主张。

2. The man of noble character devotes himself to the fundamentals

【Source】

Youzi said, "The man of noble character devotes himself to the fundamentals. When the fundamentals are established, the principles of ruling the country and conducting oneself will be formed. The fundamental of being humane lies in fulfilling filial duties to one's parents and obeying one's elder brothers."

The Analects· Xue Er Chapter1.2

【Comments】

Confucianism holds the belief that filial piety to one's parents and other elder members of the family and fraternal love to one's siblings are the fundamental of humaneness and of all the virtues based on love.

2. 君子务本

【原文】

有子曰:"君子务本,本立而道生。孝弟也者,其为仁之本与!"

《论语·学而》1.2 章

【释文】

有子说:"君子专心致力于根本的事务,根本建立了,治国做人的原则也就有了。孝顺父母、顺从兄长,这就是仁的根本啊!"

【解析】

孝是指对父母长辈的敬爱,悌是指对兄弟姐妹的友爱。儒家认为,孝悌是仁德的根本,是建立在爱心基础上的各种美德的根基。

吾日三省吾身
I examine myself several times a day

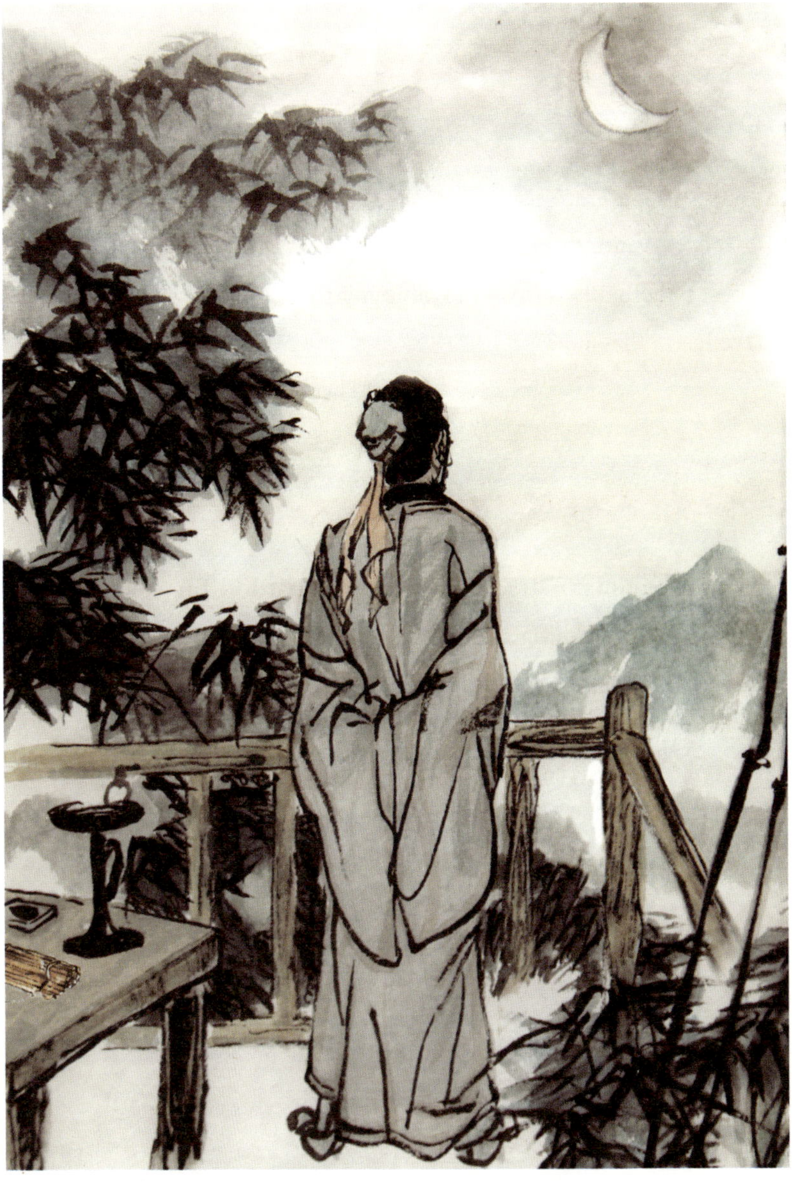

3. I examine myself several times a day

【Source】

Zengzi said, "I examine myself several times a day. Have I tried my best to help others? Am I loyal to my friends? Have I reviewed what I have learnt that day?"

The *Analects* ·Xue Er Chapter1.4

【Comments】

Confucianism stresses on self-cultivation for shaping ideal personality. Examining oneself mentioned in the Chapter is a basic method of self-cultivation and self-discipline.

3. 吾日三省吾身

【原文】

曾子曰:"吾日三省吾身:为人谋而不忠乎?与朋友交而不信乎?传不习乎?"

《论语·学而》1.4 章

【释文】

曾子说:"我每天多次反省自己:为别人办事是不是尽心竭力了呢?同朋友交往是不是做到诚实可信了呢?老师传授给我的学业是不是复习了呢?"

【解析】

儒家十分重视个人的道德修养,以塑造理想人格。本章所讲的自省,是自我修养的基本方法,体现了严于律己的精神。

4. Fulfill their filial duties at home and obey their elder brothers when away from home

【Source】

The master said, "The young should fulfill their filial duties at home and obey their elder brothers when away from home. They should be discreet, trustworthy and love the public and approach the humane. If they have the strength to spare after practicing all the above, they should learn classics."

The Analects ·Xue Er Chapter1.6

【Comments】

Confucius asked his disciples to fulfill filial duties, show respects for their elder brothers, love the public and approach the humane and cultivate morality. When they had the time and strength to spare after practicing the above, they should learn classics to increase their knowledge. It's a fine tradition in ancient China to put moral education first. Moral education of Confucius is centered on humaneness and love.

4. 入则孝，出则弟

【原文】

子曰："弟子入则孝，出则弟，谨而信，泛爱众，而亲仁，行有余力，则以学文。"

《论语·学而》1.6 章

【释文】

孔子说："年轻人在父母跟前孝顺父母，出门在外顺从师长，言行要谨慎，要诚实守信，要广泛地去爱众人，亲近那些有仁德的人。这样躬行实践之后，还有余力的话，就再去学习文献知识。"

【解析】

孔子要求弟子们首先要致力于孝悌、谨信、爱众、亲仁，培养良好的道德观念和道德行为，如果还有闲暇时间和余力，则用以学习古代典籍，增长文化知识。把道德教育放在首位，是中国古代教育的优良传统。孔子的道德教育，以"仁爱"为中心。

5.Value virtues more than lust upon a young woman

【Source】

　　Zixia said, "If a person values virtues more than lust upon a young woman, if a person does his utmost to look after his parents, if a person is willing to sacrifice his life for the sake of serving his sovereign, if a person stands by his words when dealing with his friends, I must say he is learned even though he has not learnt."

The Analects ·Xue Er Chapter1.7

【Comments】

　　Zixia believed that the main criteria of a learned person lied not in what he learnt, but in whether he had traditional morals like filial piety, loyalty and trustworthiness. If he did, he was a well-educated person even though he did not learn any cultural knowledge.

5. 贤贤易色

【原文】

子夏曰:"贤贤易色;事父母,能竭其力;事君,能致其身;与朋友交,言而有信。虽曰未学,吾必谓之学矣。"

《论语·学而》1.7 章

【释文】

子夏说:"一个人能够看重贤德而不以女色为重;侍奉父母,能够竭尽全力;服侍君主,能够献出自己的生命;同朋友交往,说话诚实恪守信用。这样的人,尽管他自己说没有学习过,我一定说他已经学习过了。"

【解析】

子夏认为,一个人有没有学问,他的学问的好坏,主要不是看他的文化知识,而是要看他能不能实行"孝"、"忠"、"信"等传统伦理道德。只要做到了后面几点,即使他说自己没有学习过,但他已经是有道德修养的人了。

慎终追远

Carefully attend to the funeral rites of one's parents
and earnestly worship one's ancestors

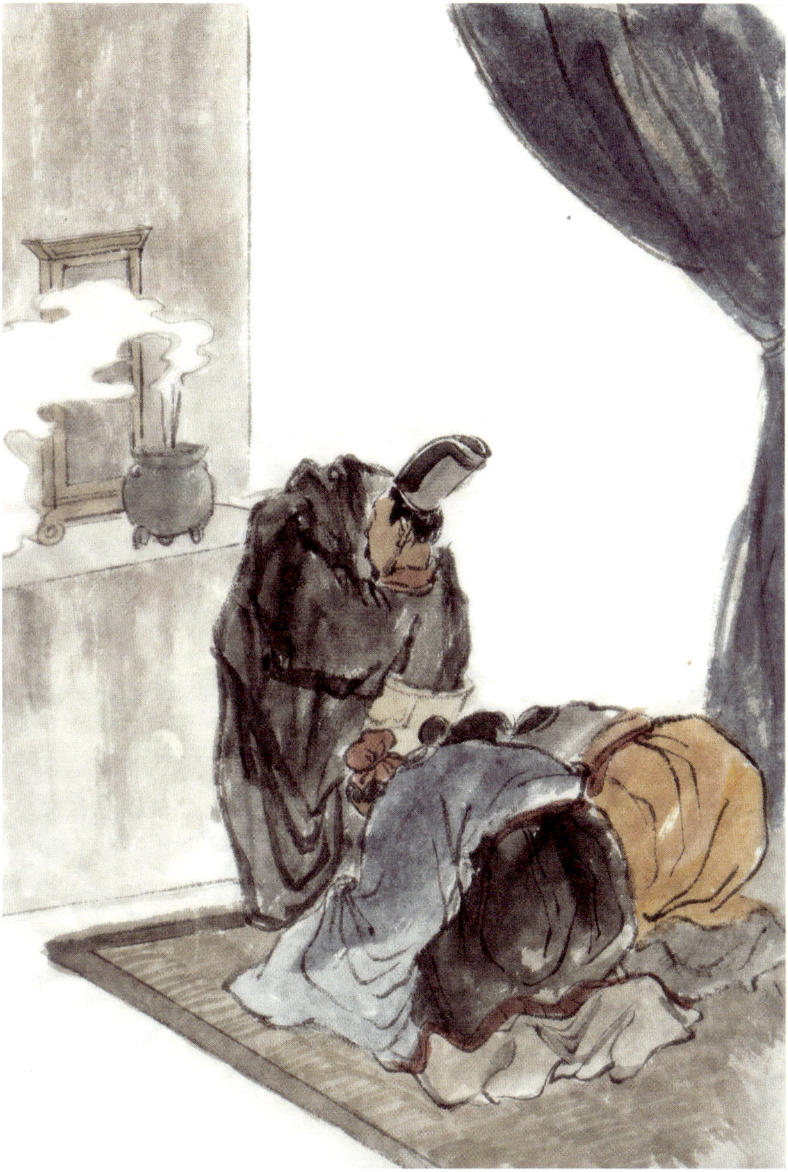

6. Carefully attend to the funeral rites of one's parents and earnestly worship one's ancestors

【Source】

Zengzi said, "When carefully attend to the funeral rites of one's parents and earnestly worship one's ancestors, the morals of common people will be greatly improved."

The Analects· Xue Er Chapter1.9

【Comments】

Confucianism believes that carefully attending to the funeral rites of one's parents and earnestly worshiping one's ancestors are the embodiment of fulfilling one's filial duties. The virtues of loyalty, reciprocity, trustworthiness, patriotism and love of one's people will be cultivated on the basis of filial piety. A person who's not filial is hard to be patriotic and loyal. Therefore, loyalty is the extension of filial piety.

6. 慎终追远

【原文】

曾子曰:"慎终追远,民德归厚矣。"

《论语·学而》1.9 章

【释文】

曾子说:"谨慎地对待父母的去世,追念祖先的功绩,自然会使老百姓的道德风气归于淳厚。"

【解析】

慎终追远是恪守孝道的体现。儒家认为,将孝敬父母的爱心扩展开来,就会培养起忠恕诚信、爱国爱民等美德。一个不能对父母尽孝的人,是难于为国尽忠的。所以忠是孝的延伸和外化。

7. Gentleness, kindness, courtesy, restraint and magnanimity

【Source】

　　Ziqin asked Zigong, "The master is able to know the political affairs with ease upon arriving in a state. Does the master make inquiry about them or do the sovereigns voluntarily tell the master about them?"

　　Zigong answered, "The master is gentle, kind, courteous, restrained and magnanimous, so he is worthy of knowing them with ease. I guess he resorts to a different way."

The Analects ·Xue Er Chapter1.10

【Comments】

　　The chapter depicts the moral character of Confucius through the dialogue between Ziqin and Zigong, which is featured by gentleness, kindness, courtesy, restraint and magnanimity.

7. 温良恭俭让

【原文】

　　子禽问于子贡曰:"夫子至于是邦也,必闻其政,求之与,抑与之与?"子贡曰:"夫子温良恭俭让以得之。夫子之求之也,其诸异乎人之求之与?"

《论语·学而》1.10 章

【释文】

　　子禽问子贡说:"老师到了一个国家,总是预闻这个国家的政事。这种资格是他自己求得呢,还是人家国君主动给他的呢?"子贡说:"老师温良恭俭让,所以才得到这样的资格。他求的方法,或许与别人的求法不同吧?"

【解析】

　　本章通过子禽与子贡两人的对话,把孔子为人处世的道德品格勾画出来:温和、善良、恭敬、俭朴、谦让。

礼之用，和为贵
In the practice of rites, harmony is to be prized

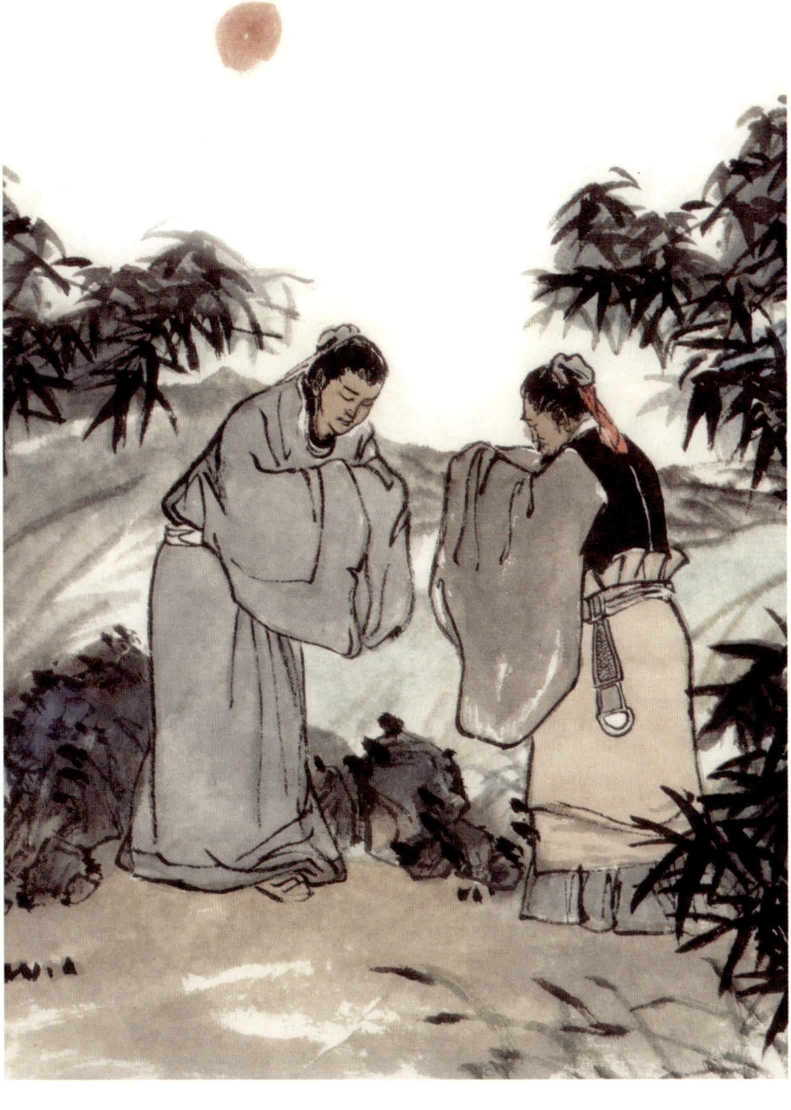

8. In the practice of rites, harmony is to be prized

【Source】

　　Youzi said, "In the practice of rites, harmony is to be prized. It is the most important aspect for the ancient sovereigns to rule their countries. However, it doesn't work sometimes if all the things, big and small, are done in a harmonious way. Seeking harmony for its own sake without regulating it with rites is a nonstarter."

The Analects ·Xue Er Chapter1.12

【Comments】

　　Harmony is a specially advocated principle of ethics, politics and society by Confucianism. Harmony should be valued in promotion and practice of rites. Nonetheless, Confucius pointed out that harmony should be regulated by rites.

8. 礼之用，和为贵

【原文】

有子曰："礼之用，和为贵。先王之道，斯为美。小大由之，有所不行。知和而和，不以礼节之，亦不可行也。"

《论语·学而》1.12 章

【释文】

有子说："礼的应用，以和谐为贵。古代君主的治国方法，可宝贵的地方就在这里。但不论大事小事只顾按和谐的办法去做，有的时候就行不通。为和谐而和谐，不以礼来节制和谐，也是不可行的。"

【解析】

"和"是儒家所特别倡导的伦理、政治和社会原则。礼的推行和应用要以和谐为贵。但孔子又指出不能为"和"而"和"，要以礼节制。

9. The person is poor, but finds delight in pursuing knowledge, or rich, but observing the rites

【Source】

Zigong asked, "Suppose a person is poor but not obsequious, or rich but not arrogant. Is it enough?"

Confucius answered, "It's good, but it'll be better if the person is poor, but finds delight in pursuing knowledge, or rich, but observing the rites."

The *Analects*· Xue Er Chapter1.15

【Comments】

Confucius hoped that his disciples and all the others could reach the ideal state of finding delight in pursuing knowledge in spite of poverty and observing the rites in spite of wealth. With this in mind, Confucius integrated the ideal state into his teaching.

9. 贫而乐，富而好礼

【原文】

子贡曰："贫而无谄，富而无骄，何如？"子曰："可也。未若贫而乐，富而好礼者也。"

《论语·学而》1.15 章

【释文】

子贡说："贫穷而能不谄媚，富有而能不骄傲自大，怎么样？"孔子说："这也算可以了。但是还不如虽贫穷却乐于求道，虽富裕而又好礼之人。"

【解析】

孔子希望他的弟子以及所有的人，都能够达到贫而乐道、富而好礼这样的理想境界，因而在平时对弟子的教育中，就把这样的思想讲授给学生。

为政以德

Rule a country on the basis of morality

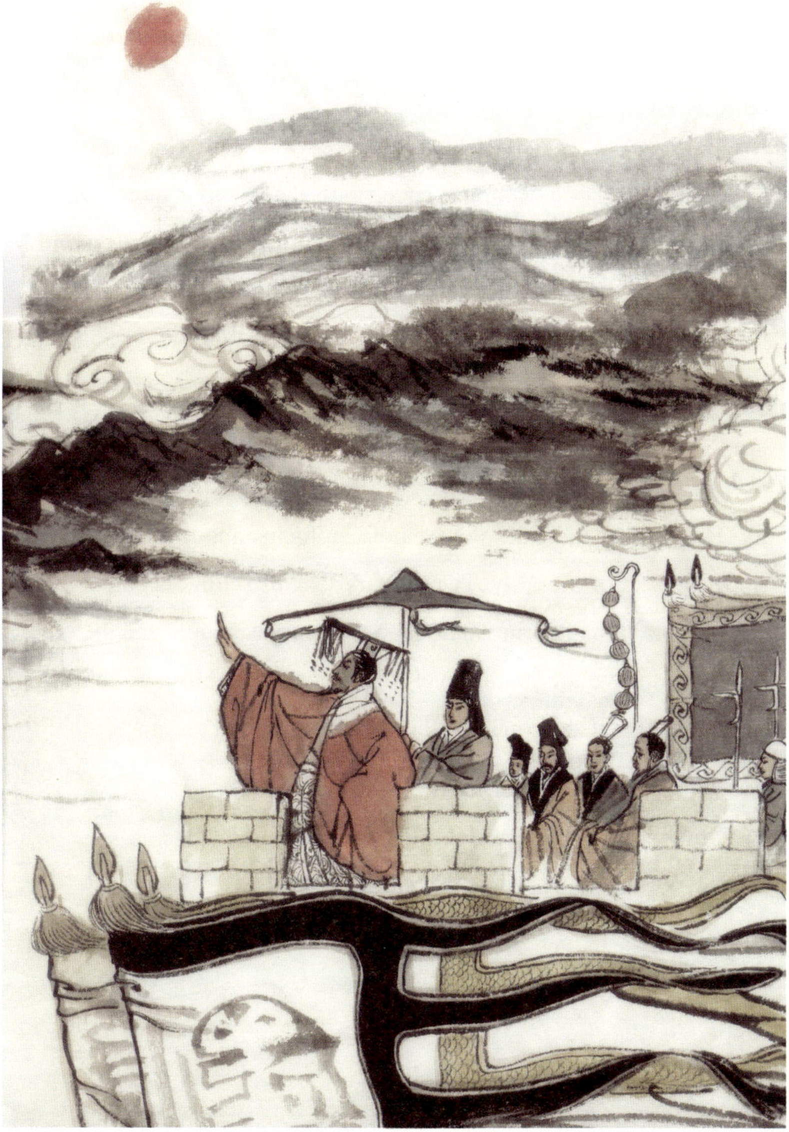

10.Rule a country on the basis of morality

【Source】

Confucius said, "Ruling a country on the basis of morality is like the Pole Star, which is situated in its position while moved around by other stars."

The *Analects* ·Wei Zheng Chapter2.1

【Comments】

The chapter indicates the idea of Confucius about ruling a country with the power of morality. The primary task of ruling a country on the basis of morality is to bring material benefits to its people and the second one is to improve the moral level of the general public by focusing on moral education. Consequently, the society will be in order and stability.

10. 为政以德

【原文】

子曰:"为政以德,譬如北辰,居其所而众星共之。"

《论语·为政》2.1 章

【释文】

孔子说:"以德来治理政事,就会像北极星那样,自己居于一定的位置,而群星都会环绕在它的周围。"

【解析】

本章表明了孔子"为政以德"的思想。"德治"的首要任务是在物质上给民众以恩惠(惠民),其次,在精神上执政者要提高道德修养(爱民),并重视对民众的道德教育(化民)。这样做,天下就会大治。

11. The general public is directed by moral education and constrained by rites

【Source】

The master said, "If the general public is directed by laws and regulations and constrained by penalty, they may not commit crimes, but will not feel ashamed of their wrongdoings. On the contrary, if the general public is directed by moral education and constrained by rites, they will not only abide by rules, but also have sense of shame."

The *Analects* ·Wei Zheng Chapter2.3

【Comments】

In this chapter, Confucius enumerated two completely different ways of ruling a country. Confucius believed that penalty could refrain a person from committing a crime, but not help him feel ashamed of committing it while moral education could attain the both goals.

11. 道之以德，齐之以礼

【原文】

子曰："道之以政，齐之以刑，民免而无耻；道之以德，齐之以礼，有耻且格。"

《论语·为政》2.3 章

【释文】

孔子说："用法制禁令去引导百姓，使用刑法来约束他们，老百姓只是求得免于犯罪受惩，却失去了廉耻之心；用道德教化引导百姓，使用礼制去统一百姓的言行，百姓不仅会有羞耻之心，而且也就守规矩了。"

【解析】

在本章，孔子举出两种截然不同的治国方针。孔子认为，刑罚只能使人避免犯罪，不能使人懂得犯罪可耻的道理，而道德教化比刑罚要高明得多，既能使百姓守规蹈矩，又能使百姓有知耻之心。

12. Establish myself at 30 and have no doubts about the world at 40

【Source】

The master said, "I made the decision to devote myself to learning at 15, and established myself at 30. I had no doubts about the world at 40. I knew my destiny at 50 and I could distinguish right and wrong in other people's words at 60. Since 70, I have followed my inclinations without transgressing."

The *Analects* ·Wei Zheng Chapter2.4

【Comments】

In this chapter, Confucius recounted his journey of learning and self-cultivation. His moral level increased with the increase of age during the journey.

12. 三十而立，四十而不惑

【原文】

子曰："吾十有五而志于学，三十而立，四十而不惑，五十而知天命，六十而耳顺，七十而从心所欲不逾矩。"

《论语·为政》2.4 章

【释文】

孔子说："我十五岁立志于学习；三十岁能够自立；四十岁能不被外界事物所迷惑；五十岁懂得了天命；六十岁能正确对待各种言论，不觉得不顺；七十岁能随心所欲而不越出规矩。"

【解析】

在本章，孔子自述了他学习和修养的过程。这一过程，是一个随着年龄增长，思想境界逐步提高的过程。

温故而知新

Derive new reflections from reviewing what one's learnt

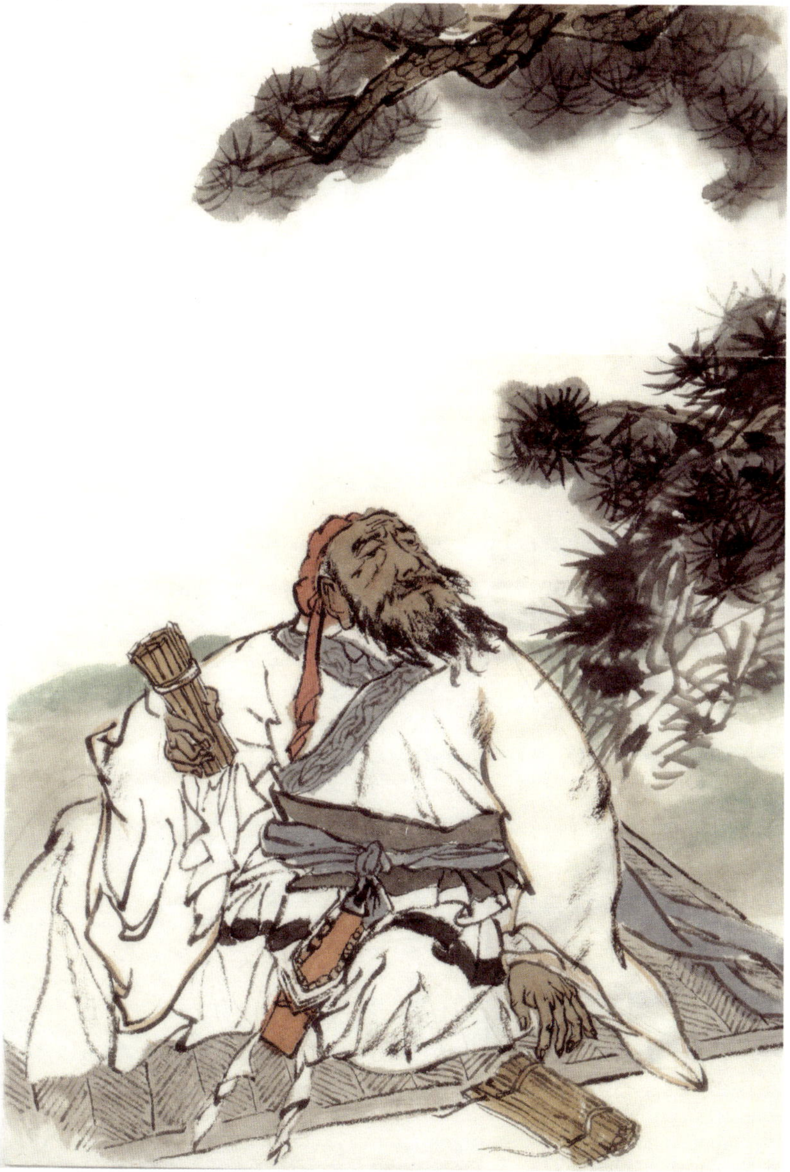

13. Derive new reflections from reviewing what one's learnt

【Source】

The master said, "One can be a teacher if he derives new reflections from reviewing what he's learnt."

The Analects ·Wei Zheng Chapter2.11

【Comments】

New knowledge is built upon what one has learnt. It's universal law of learning to get new reflections from what one has learnt and also a goal one should strive to attain in his learning.

13. 温故而知新

【原文】

子曰:"温故而知新,可以为师矣。"

《论语·为政》2.11 章

【释文】

孔子说:"温习旧知识而有新体会、新发现,就可以当老师了。"

【解析】

人们的新知识、新学问往往是在过去所学知识的基础上发展而来的,温故而知新是一个读书学习的普遍规律,也是读书人求学应当努力实现的目标。

学而不思则罔，思而不学则殆

He who is steeped in learning but neglecting thinking feels perplexed while he who is absorbed in thinking but neglecting learning puts himself in danger

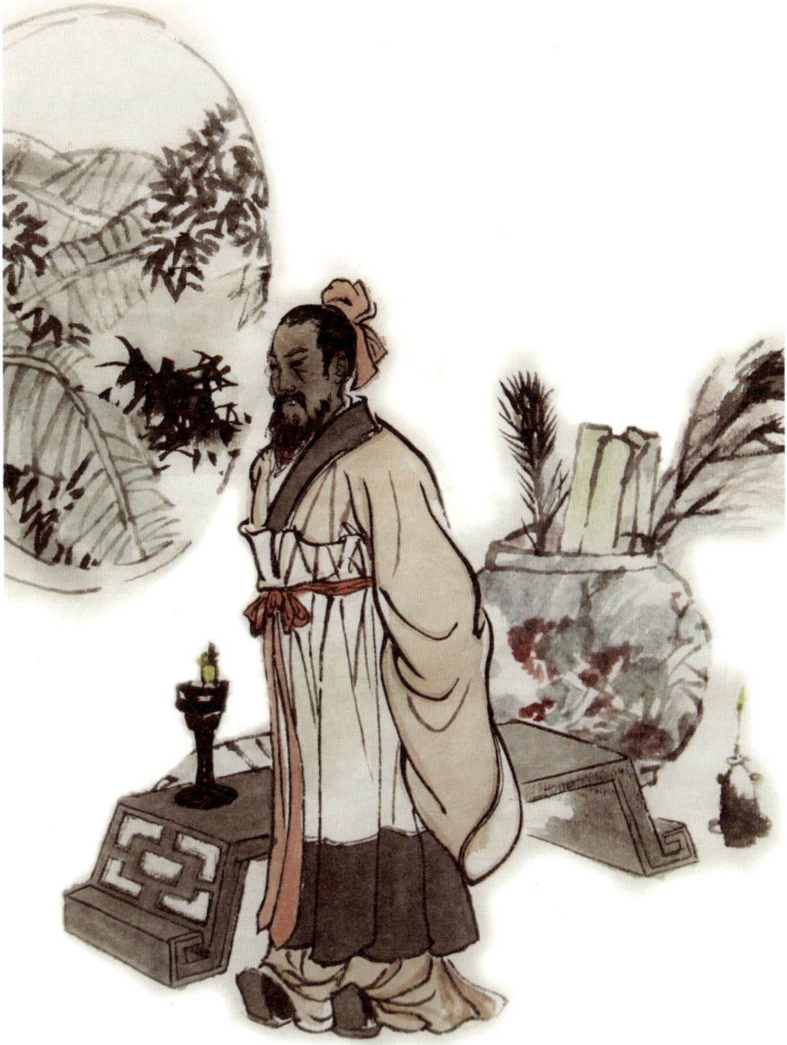

14. He who is steeped in learning but neglecting thinking feels perplexed while he who is absorbed in thinking but neglecting learning puts himself in danger

【Source】

The master said, "He who is steeped in learning but neglecting thinking feels perplexed while he who is absorbed in thinking but neglecting learning puts himself in danger."

The Analects ·Wei Zheng Chapter 2.15

【Comments】

Confucius believed that learning and thinking were two sides of one coin. He pointed out the constraints of learning without thinking and the dangers of thinking without learning and stressed the importance of combining both in the course of obtaining knowledge.

14. 学而不思则罔，思而不学则殆

【原文】

子曰："学而不思则罔，思而不学则殆。"

《论语·为政》2.15 章

【释文】

孔子说："只读书学习而不思考问题，就会惘然无知而没有收获；只空想而不读书学习，就会疑惑而难定夺。"

【解析】

孔子认为，在学习的过程中，学和思不能偏废。他指出了学而不思的局限，也道出了思而不学的弊端，主张学与思相结合。

15. Say yes when you know and no when you don't, it's the wisdom

【Source】

The master said, "You, do you understand what I taught you? Say yes when you know and no when you don't, it's the wisdom."

The *Analects* ·Wei Zheng Chapter2.17

【Comments】

People should work hard at learning and try their best to master as much knowledge as they can. Nonetheless, they are not masters of all professions. When admitting the fact, they are capable of learning more knowledge.

15. 知之为知之，不知为不知，是知也

【原文】

子曰："由，诲女知之乎？知之为知之，不知为不知，是知也。"

《论语·为政》2.17 章

【释文】

孔子说："由，我教给你的你明白了吗？知道就是知道，不知道就是不知道，这就是智慧啊！"

【解析】

人们对各种知识应刻苦学习，尽可能多地加以掌握，但总会碰到不懂的问题，因而应当有实事求是的态度，才能学到更多的知识。

言寡尤，行寡悔，禄在其中矣

With fewer mistakes in your words and fewer regrets in your deeds, you can obtain a government position and receive an official's salary

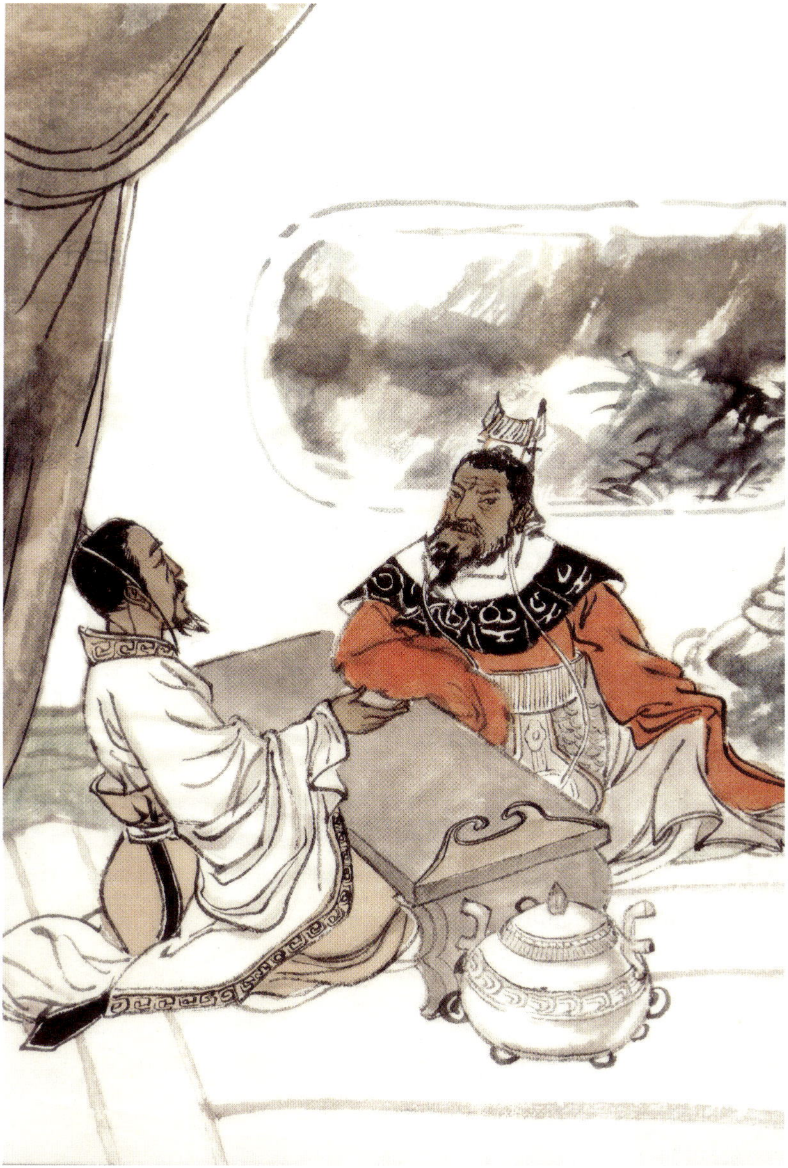

16. With fewer mistakes in your words and fewer regrets in your deeds, you can obtain a government position and receive an official's salary

【Source】

Zizhang asked the master about how to obtain a government position. The master said, "Use your ears to listen. Do not say what you are uncertain of and be cautious about saying what you are certain of. Thus, you can reduce your mistakes. Use your eyes to see. Do not do what your are uncertain of and be cautious about doing what you are certain of. Thus you can reduce your regrets. With fewer mistakes in your words and fewer regrets in your deeds, you can obtain a government position and receive an official's salary."

The *Analects* ·Wei Zheng Chapter2.18

【Comments】

Confucius deemed that an official should be discreet and say and do only what he's certain of to reduce mistakes and regrets. It's a responsible attitude for the country and its people.

16. 言寡尤，行寡悔，禄在其中矣

【原文】

子张学干禄。子曰："多闻阙疑，慎言其余，则寡尤；多见阙殆，慎行其余，则寡悔。言寡尤，行寡悔，禄在其中矣。"

《论语·为政》2.18 章

【释文】

子张要学谋取官职的办法。孔子说："要多听，有怀疑的地方先放在一旁不说，其余有把握的，也要谨慎地说出来，这样就可以少犯错误；要多看，有怀疑的地方先放在一旁不做，其余有把握的，也要谨慎地去做，这样就可以减少后悔。说话少过失，做事少后悔，官职俸禄就在其中了。"

【解析】

孔子认为，身居官位者，应当谨言慎行，说有把握的话，做有把握的事，这样可以减少失误，减少后悔。这是对国家对个人负责任的态度。

人而无信，不知其可也
An untrustworthy person cannot establish himself in the world

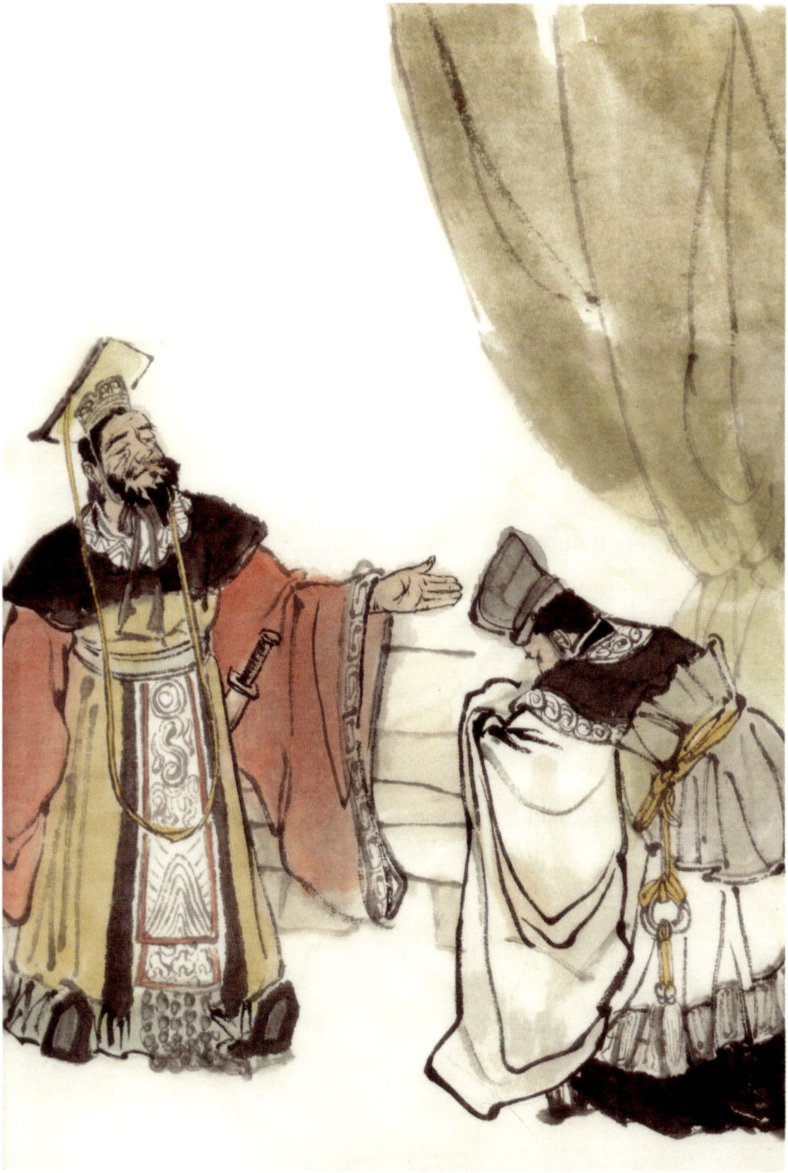

17. An untrustworthy person cannot establish himself in the world

【Source】

The master said, "An untrustworthy person cannot establish himself in the world. It's like a carriage with no wheels, can it move?"

The *Analects* ·Wei Zheng Chapter2.22

【Comments】

Confucius thought that trustworthiness was the basis for a person to establish himself in the world. Trustworthiness covers the following two meanings. First, officials should win the trust of the people. Second, a common person should keep his words.

17. 人而无信，不知其可也

【原文】

子曰："人而无信，不知其可也。大车无輗，小车无軏，其何以行之哉？"

《论语·为政》2.22章

【释文】

孔子说："一个人不诚信，不知道他在社会上怎么行得通。就好像大车没有輗、小车没有軏一样，它靠什么行走呢？"

【解析】

孔子认为，信是人立身处世的基点。信的含义有两种：一是信任，如为官当取信于民，让民众信任自己；二是对人诚信，讲信用。

18. what is subtracted and added is knowable

【Source】

Zizhang asked the master, "Is it possible to know the state of affairs ten generations hence?"

The Master answered, "Shang Dynasty based its rite system on that of Xia Dynasty, so what is subtracted and added is knowable. Zhou Dynasty based its rite system on that of Shang Dynasty, so what is subtracted and added is knowable. The state of affairs ten generations hence is also knowable if the future generations base their rite system on that of Zhou Dynasty."

The *Analects* ·Wei Zheng Chapter2.23

【Comments】

In this chapter, Confucius put forward a crucial concept: what is subtracted and added. It refers to both inheritance and reforms of institutions and rites of the previous dynasty.

18. 损益可知

【原文】

子张问"十世可知也？"子曰"殷因于夏礼，所损益可知也周因于殷礼，所损益可知也。其或继周者，虽百世，可知也。"

《论语·为政》2.23 章

【释文】

子张问孔子："今后十世可以预先知道吗？"孔子回答说："商朝继承了夏朝的礼仪制度，所废除和所增加的内容是可以知道的；周朝又继承商朝的礼仪制度，所废除和所增加的内容也是可以知道的。将来有继承周朝的，就是一百世以后的情况，也是可以预先知道的。"

【解析】

在本章，孔子提出一个重要概念：损益。它的含义是增减、兴革。即对前代典章制度、礼仪规范等有继承、沿袭，也有改革、变通。

19. How can a person with no humaneness observe rites

【Source】

The master said, "How can a person with no humaneness observe rites? How can a person with no humaneness use music in a proper way?"

The *Analects* ·Ba Yi Chapter3.3

【Comments】

Confucius combined rites with humaneness and music. He believed that humaneness was the moral requirement and rites and music were outward expression. A person with no humaneness can not observe rites or use music in a proper way.

19. 人而不仁，如礼何

【原文】

子曰："人而不仁，如礼何？人而不仁，如乐何？"

《论语·八佾》3.3 章

【释文】

孔子说："一个人没有仁德，他怎么能实行礼呢？一个人没有仁德，他怎么能运用乐呢？"

【解析】

孔子把礼、乐与仁紧紧联系起来，认为仁是人们内心的道德情感和要求，礼与乐是外在的表现，没有仁德的人，根本谈不上施行礼、乐。

礼，与其奢也，宁俭

Being economical is better than extravagant at ritual ceremonies

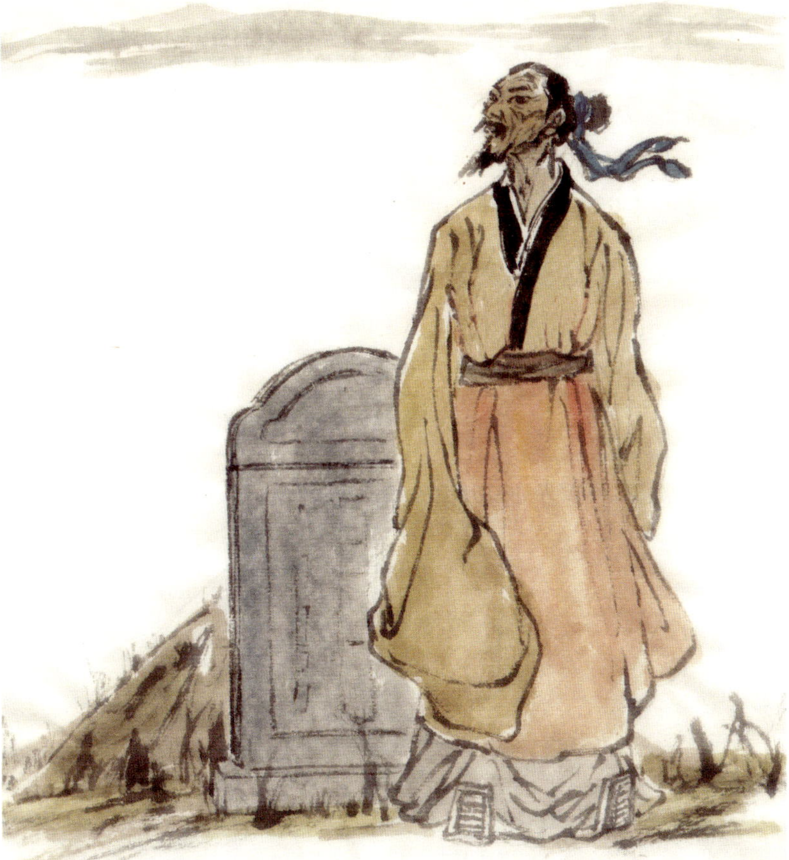

20. Being economical is better than extravagant at ritual ceremonies

【Source】

Lin Fang asked the master about the fundamental of rites. The master said, "Your question is of profound meaning. Being economical is better than extravagant at ritual ceremonies. Feeling mournful is better than a well-arranged ceremony at the funeral."

The *Analects* ·Ba Yi Chapter3.4

【Comments】

Confucius believed that the fundamental of rites was not its form, but its substance. One should not stay on the surface when practicing rites. He should understand the fundamental of rites and conform to the requirements of rites. The fundamental of rites is humaneness.

20. 礼，与其奢也，宁俭

【原文】

林放问礼之本。子曰："大哉问！礼，与其奢也，宁俭；丧，与其易也，宁戚。"

《论语·八佾》3.4 章

【释文】

林放问什么是礼的根本。孔子回答说："你问的问题意义重大呀！礼节仪式，与其奢侈，不如节俭；丧事，与其仪式上治办周备，不如内心真正哀伤。"

【解析】

孔子认为，礼的根本不在形式而在内心，遵礼不能只停留在表面仪式上，更重要的是要从内心和感情上体悟礼的根本，符合礼的要求。礼的根本在"仁"。

21. The ruler should use his ministers in accordance with rites and his ministers should serve his ruler with loyalty

【Source】

Duke Ding of the State of Lu asked the master, "how should a ruler use his ministers and how should his ministers serve his ruler?"

The master answered, "The ruler should use his ministers in accordance with rites and his ministers should serve his ruler with loyalty."

The *Analects* ·Ba Yi Chapter3.19

【Comments】

The relationship between a ruler and his ministers will be in harmony and the practice of government will be on the right track when the ruler uses his ministers in accordance with rites and his ministers serve the ruler with loyalty.

21. 君使臣以礼，臣事君以忠

【原文】

定公问："君使臣，臣事君，如之何？"孔子对曰："君使臣以礼，臣事君以忠。"

《论语·八佾》3.19 章

【释文】

鲁定公问："君主使用臣子，臣子事奉君主，该怎么做呢？"孔子回答说："君主应该按照礼的要求使用臣子，臣子应该以忠来事奉君主。"

【解析】

君主礼敬臣子，臣子忠诚于君主，做到这样，君臣关系才会和谐，政治才会走上正道。

君子无终食之间违仁

The man of noble character will never deviate from humaneness
for even the time of a simple meal

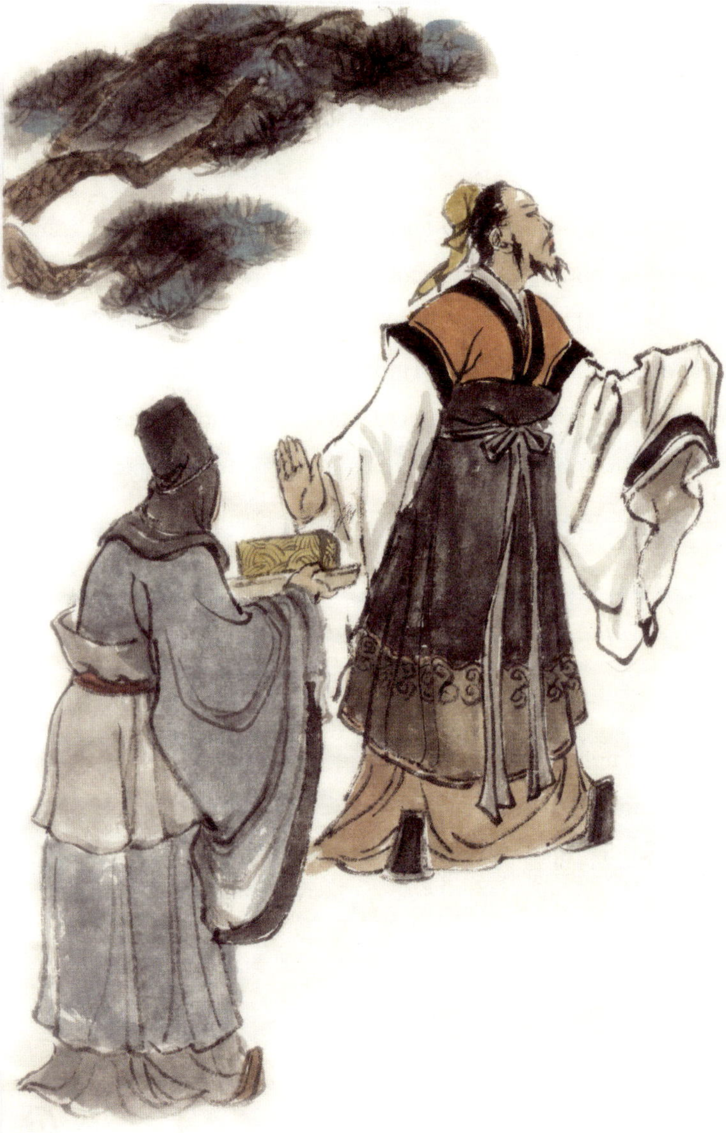

22. The man of noble character will never deviate from humaneness for even the time of a simple meal

【Source】

The master said, "Wealth and high rank are desired by all, but I don't want them both if they are acquired by improper ways. Poverty and lowliness are hated by all. But I would rather keep them both if they are gotten rid of in an improper way. How can a person with no humaneness become the man of noble character? The man of noble character will never deviate from humaneness for even the time of a simple meal, nor in the direst moments or when displaced."

The Analects ·Li Ren Chapter4.5

【Comments】

No one intends to live a poor and displaced life. All desire for rich and comfortable life. Nonetheless, wealth and high rank should be acquired through proper ways. Otherwise, it's better to live in poverty.

22. 君子无终食之间违仁

【原文】

子曰:"富与贵,是人之所欲也,不以其道得之,不处也;贫与贱,是人之所恶也,不以其道得之,不去也。君子去仁,恶乎成名?君子无终食之间违仁,造次必于是,颠沛必于是。"

《论语·里仁》4.5 章

【释文】

孔子说:"富裕和显贵是人人都想要得到的,但不用正当的方法得到它,就不去享受;贫穷与低贱是人人都厌恶的,但不用正当的方法去摆脱它,就不去摆脱。君子如果离开了仁德,又怎么能叫君子呢?君子没有一顿饭的时间背离仁德,就是在最紧迫的时刻也必须按照仁德办事,就是在颠沛流离的时候也必须按照仁德办事。"

【解析】

任何人都不会甘愿过贫穷困顿、流离失所的生活,都希望得到富贵安逸,但这必须通过正当的手段和途径去获取,否则宁守清贫而不去享受富贵。

朝闻道，夕死可矣
If I know the Way in the morning, I can die without regrets at night

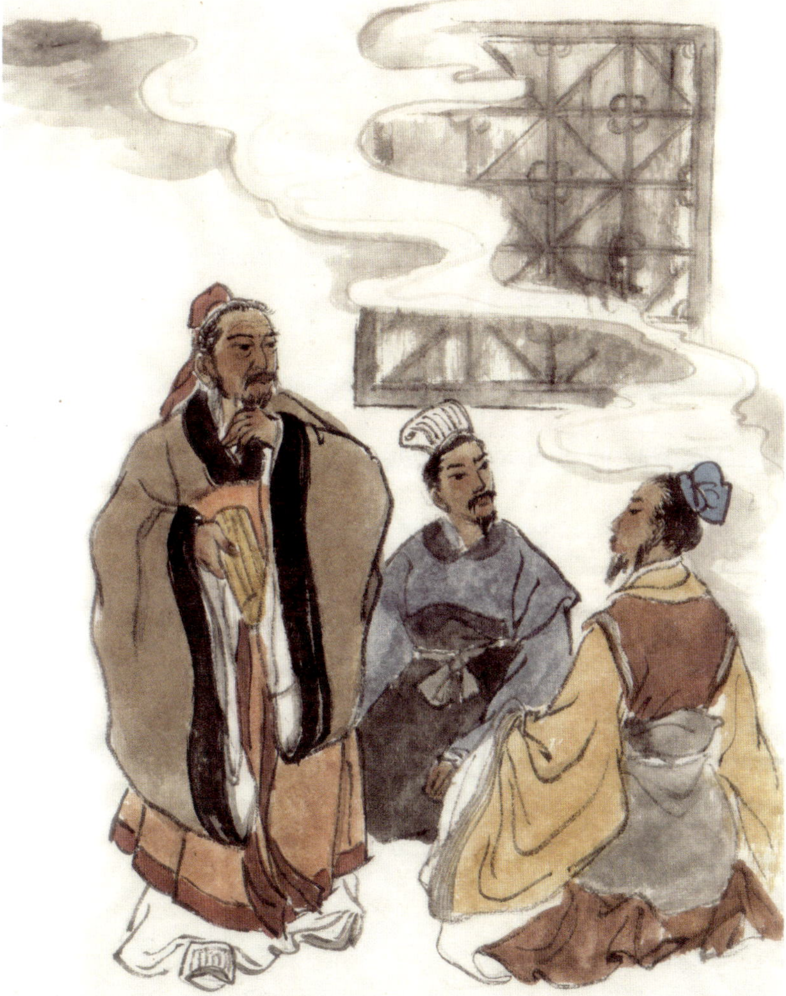

23.If I know the Way in the morning, I can die without regrets at night

【Source】

The master said, "If I know the Way in the morning, I can die without regrets at night."

The *Analects* ·Li Ren Chapter4.8

【Comments】

The Way mentioned by Confucius refers to the supreme ethic principles of regulating a society and ruling a country and the highest moral standard for a person.

23. 朝闻道，夕死可矣

【原文】

子曰："朝闻道，夕死可矣。"

《论语·里仁》4.8 章

【释文】

孔子说："早晨得知了道，就是当天晚上死去也心甘。"

【解析】

孔子这里所讲的"道"，是指社会、政治的最高原则和做人的最高准则，这主要是从伦理学意义上说的。

24. The man of noble character takes action in accordance with righteousness

【Source】

The master said, "There are no certain rules for the man of noble character to do, nor are there certain restricts for him not to do. The Man of noble character takes action in accordance with righteousness."

The Analects ·Li Ren Chapter4.10

【Comments】

Confucius held the belief that action should be taken in accordance with the local conditions and expediency was allowable. However, expediency should be based upon righteousness.

24. 义之与比

【原文】

子曰:"君子之于天下也,无适也,无莫也,义之与比。"

《论语·里仁》4.10 章

【释文】

孔子说:"君子对于天下的事情,没有规定一定要这样做,也没有规定一定不要这样做,而是紧紧依照恰当合理的原则来做。"

【解析】

孔子主张君子做事,应因时制宜、权宜变通,但权宜变通是有准则的,即是否合理,是否符合道义。

25. One should worry not about obtaining no official positions, but about not qualified for that position

【Source】

The master said, "One should worry not about obtaining no official positions, but about not qualified for that position. One should worry not about not being recognized, but about not qualified for being recognized."

The *Analects* ·Li Ren Chapter4.14

【Comments】

It was constantly discussed by Confucius and his disciples and it's Confucius's basic attitude towards being established and his essential requirements for his disciples. It is not that Confucius did not want to be famous or occupy an important position, but that he placed great emphasis on cultivation of knowledge, moral accomplishment and talents, with which one was qualified to hold an important position.

25. 不患无位，患所以立

【原文】

子曰："不患无位，患所以立；不患莫己知，求为可知也。"

《论语·里仁》4.14 章

【释文】

孔子说："不怕没有官位，就怕自己没有学到赖以站得住脚的东西；不怕没有人知道自己，只求自己成为有真才实学能让人们知道的人。"

【解析】

这是孔子和学生经常谈论的问题，是他立身处世的基本态度，也是对学生的基本要求。孔子并非不想成名成家，并非不想身居要职，而是强调必须首先立足于自身的学问、修养、才能的培养，具备足以胜任官职的各方面素质。

吾道一以贯之

There is one main thread throughout my teaching

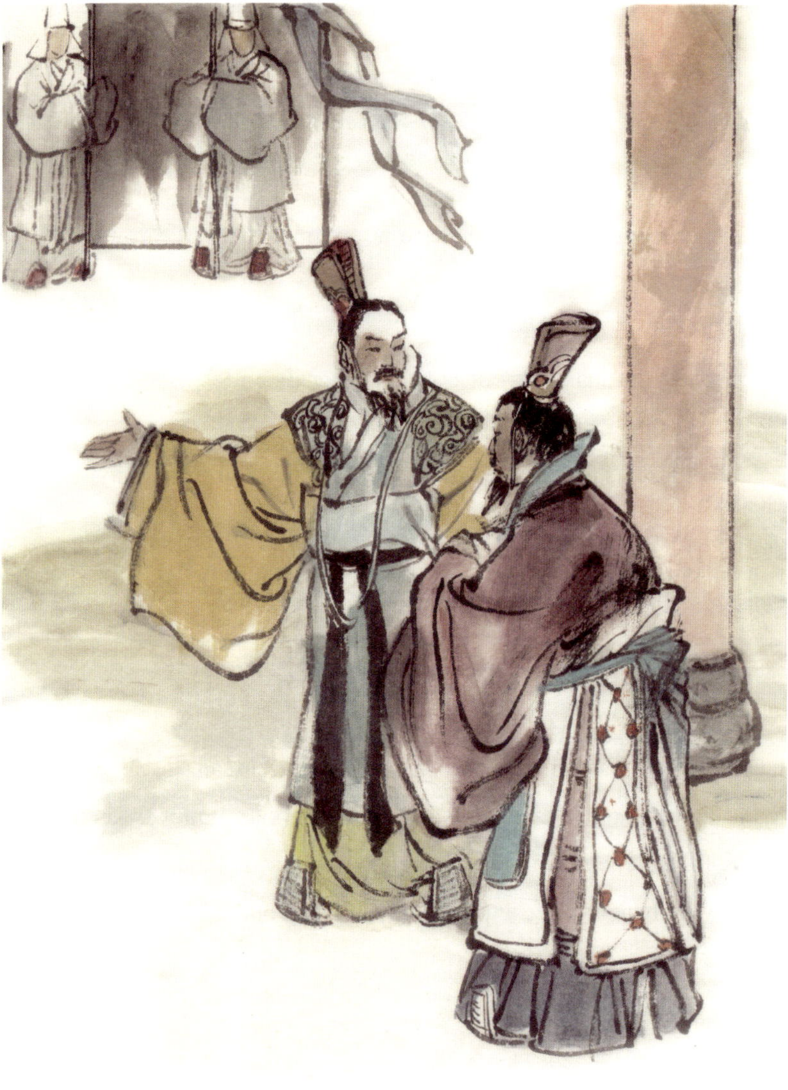

26. There is one main thread throughout my teaching

【Source】

The master said, "Cen, there is one main thread throughout my teaching."

Zeng Cen said, "Yes."

When the master went out, his other disciples asked Zeng Cen, "What does the master mean by one main thread?"

Zeng Cen said, "The main thread is loyalty and reciprocity."

The *Analects* ·Li Ren Chapter 4.15

【Comments】

The kernel of Confucius's teaching is humaneness, which is multi-faceted with loyalty and reciprocity as its main thread. Loyalty refers to being loyal to one's country, superiors, others and duties. Reciprocity refers to leniency, kindness, benevolence and magnanimity, treating others with benevolence and putting oneself in others' shoes.

26. 吾道一以贯之

【原文】

子曰:"参乎,吾道一以贯之。"曾子曰:"唯。"子出,门人问曰:"何谓也?"曾子曰:"夫子之道,忠恕而已矣。"

《论语·里仁》4.15章

【释文】

孔子说:"参啊,我的学说是由一条中心线索贯穿起来的。"曾子说:"是。"孔子出去之后,同学便问曾子:"这是什么意思?"曾子说:"他老人家的学说,就是忠恕罢了。"

【解析】

孔子学说的核心是"仁"。孔子仁学的丰富内容,又是以"忠恕"为中心线索贯穿起来的。忠是指对国家、对上司、对他人、对职事尽心尽力尽责,忠心不二。恕是指宽容、厚道、仁慈、忍让,以仁爱之心待人,能推己及人,将心比心,处处为他人着想。

27. The man of noble character understands righteousness while the mean man knows only profits

【Source】

The master said, "The man of noble character understands righteousness while the mean man knows only profits."

The *Analects* ·Li Ren Chapter4.16

【Comments】

The man of noble character differs with the mean man in views on righteousness and profits. Confucius thought that the man of noble character should value righteousness and belittle profits.

27. 君子喻于义，小人喻于利

【原文】

子曰："君子喻于义，小人喻于利。"

《论语·里仁》4.16 章

【释文】

孔子说："君子明白大义，小人只知道小利。"

【解析】

君子和小人在义利观上有所不同。孔子认为，作为君子，利要服从义，要重义轻利。

28. When you see the man with virtues, try to emulate him

【Source】

The master said, "When you see the man with virtues, try to emulate him. When you see the man without virtues, examine yourself and avoid having the same defects."

The *Analects* ·Li Ren Chapter4.17

【Comments】

The chapter discusses ways of self-cultivation. One should draw upon others' strong points to make up for his own deficiencies and learn from others' mistakes to avoid falling into the same trap.

28. 见贤思齐

【原文】

子曰:"见贤思齐焉,见不贤而内自省也。"

《论语·里仁》4.17章

【释文】

孔子说:"见到贤人,就应该向他学习、看齐,见到不贤的人,就应该自我反省有没有与他相类似的错误。"

【解析】

本章谈的是个人道德修养方法,即取别人之长补自己之短,又以别人的过失为鉴,不重蹈别人的旧辙。

事父母几谏
When waiting on parents, children should
euphemistically persuade their parents into correcting their mistakes

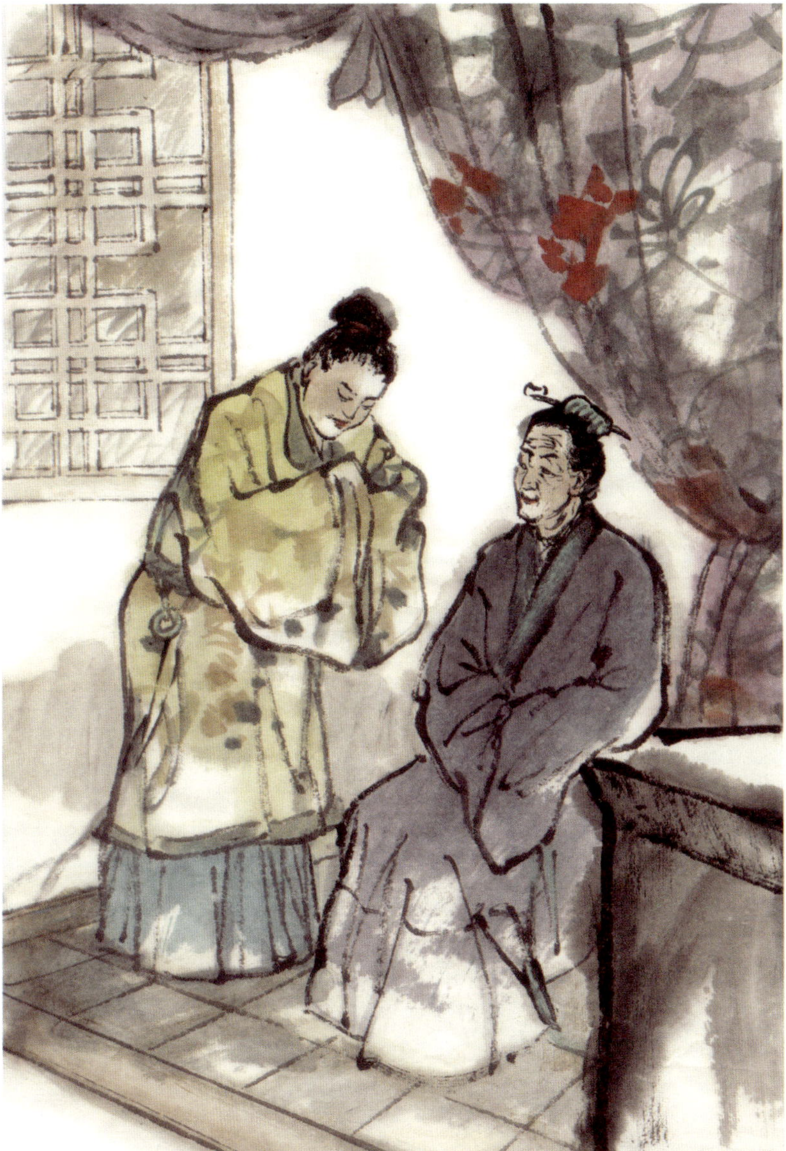

29. When waiting on parents, children should euphemistically persuade their parents into correcting their mistakes

【Source】

The master said, "When waiting on parents, children should euphemistically persuade their parents into correcting their mistakes. If their parents have no mind to give an ear to them, they should be deferential to their parents and look after them with no grudges."

The *Analects* ·Li Ren Chapter4.18

【Comments】

Confucius held the belief that children should respect their parents and euphemistically persuade their parents into correcting their mistakes. They should remain deferential to their parents no matter whether their parents give attention to their words or not.

29. 事父母几谏

【原文】

子曰:"事父母几谏,见志不从,又敬不违,劳而不怨。"

《论语·里仁》4.18 章

【释文】

孔子说:"事奉父母,如果父母有不对的地方,要委婉地劝说他们,若劝说后父母不愿听从,还是要对他们恭敬而不违抗,替他们忧虑而不怨恨。"

【解析】

孔子认为,事奉父母要孝敬,对于父母做得不对的地方,应该委婉劝告,无论父母听不听从,都不能改变对他们的恭敬。

30. Being slow to speak for fear of not suiting their deeds to their words

【Source】

The master said, "The ancient people were slow to speak for fear of not suiting their deeds to their words."

The *Analects* ·Li Ren Chapter4.22

【Comments】

Confucius thought that it was a shame not to honor one's promise and he advocated matching words with deeds, exercising caution in speech and conduct and avoiding making promises lightly.

30. 言之不出，耻躬之不逮也

【原文】

子曰："古者言之不出，耻躬之不逮也。"

《论语·里仁》4.22 章

【释文】

孔子说："古代人不轻易把话说出口，因为他们以自己做不到为可耻。"

【解析】

孔子认为不能兑现诺言是可耻的，一贯主张言行一致，谨言慎行，不轻易允诺。

31. Self-disciplined people scarcely make any mistakes

【Source】

The master said, "Self-disciplined people scarcely make any mistakes."

The *Analects* ·Li Ren Chapter4.23

【Comments】

Confucius deemed that self-discipline and caution in speech and conduct kept people away from making mistakes.

31. 以约失之者鲜矣

【原文】

子曰:"以约失之者鲜矣。"

《论语·里仁》4.23 章

【释文】

孔子说:"严格约束自己却犯错误的人很少。"

【解析】

孔子认为,约束自己,慎言慎行,就会少犯错误。

讷于言而敏于行

Being slow to speak, but quick to act

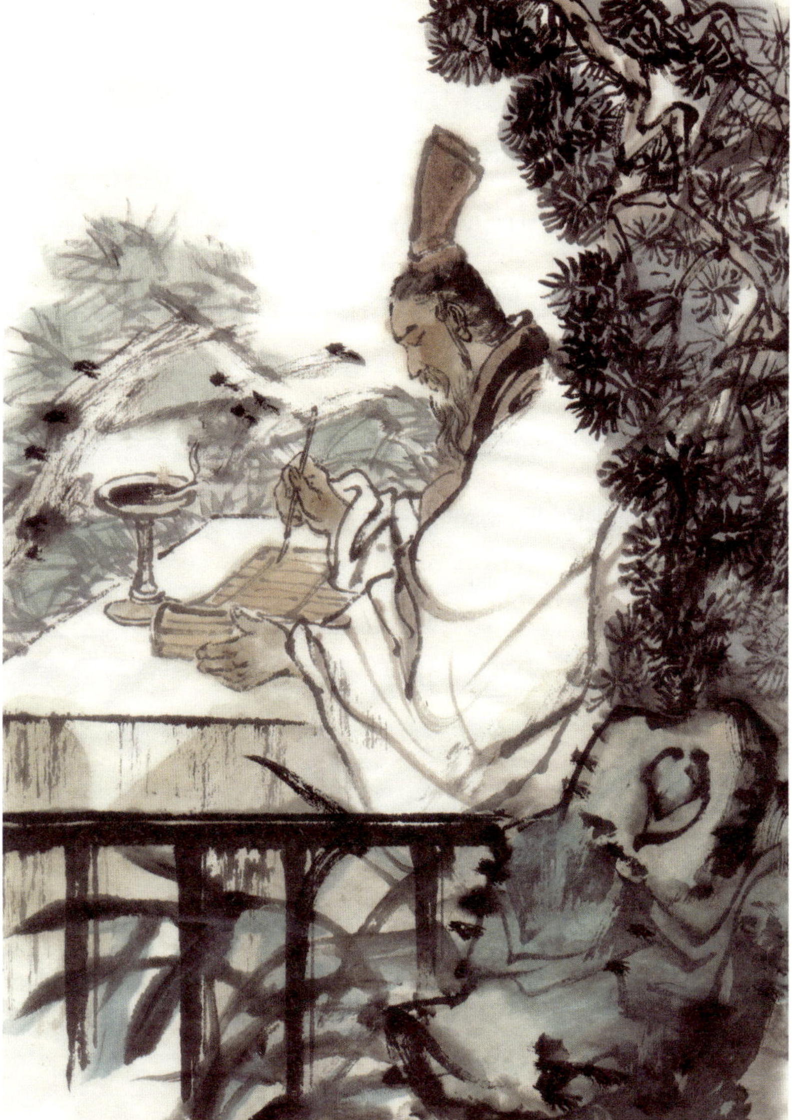

32.Being slow to speak, but quick to act

【Source】

The master said, "The man of noble character is slow to speak, but quick to act."

The *Analects* ·Li Ren Chapter4.24

【Comments】

Confucius hated those who paid lip service and advocated for hard work.

32. 讷于言而敏于行

【原文】

子曰:"君子欲讷于言而敏于行。"

《论语·里仁》4.24 章

【释文】

孔子说:"君子说话要谨慎,而行动要敏捷。"

【解析】

孔子讨厌巧言令色的人,主张勤奋肯干。

33.Infer ten things from one he has learnt

【Source】

The master asked Zigong, "Who is better, you or Yan Hui?"

Zigong answered, "How dare I compare with Yan Hui? Yan Hui can infer ten things from one he has learnt while I can only infer two from one."

The master said, "You are not on a par with Yan Hui, neither am I."

The *Analects* ·Gongye Chang Chapter5.9

【Comments】

Zigong and Yan Hui were Confucius's two top disciples. Zigong was in favor of commenting about others. In the chapter, Confucius asked Zigong to compare him with Yan Hui and Zigong thought he was no rival to Yan Hui. Confucius said he himself like Zigong, was not on a par with Yan Hui. Confucius commended Yan Hui for his intelligence and Zigong for his answer. The question and answer embodies the broad mind of Confucius and his disciple and the free and friendly communication ambience.

33. 闻一以知十

【原文】

子谓子贡曰:"女与回也孰愈?"对曰:"赐也何敢望回?回也闻一以知十,赐也闻一以知二。"子曰:"弗如也!吾与女弗如也。"

《论语·公冶长》5.9章

【释文】

孔子对子贡说:"你和颜回,哪一个强些?"子贡答道:"我怎么敢和颜回相比?颜回听到一件事,可以推演知道十件事;我呢,听到一件事,只能推演知道两件事。"孔子说:"你确实不如他,我和你一样不如他。"

【解析】

子贡和颜回都是孔子的优秀弟子。子贡常常喜欢评价别人,孔子此处让子贡自己与颜回对比,子贡自称不如颜回。孔子说自己和子贡一样不如颜回,既赞扬了颜回,也是对子贡回答的赞许。一问一答中孔门师徒博大宽广的心胸和自由融洽的交流氛围显露无遗。

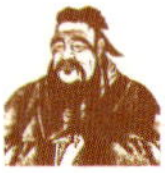

朽木不可雕也

Rotten wood cannot be carved

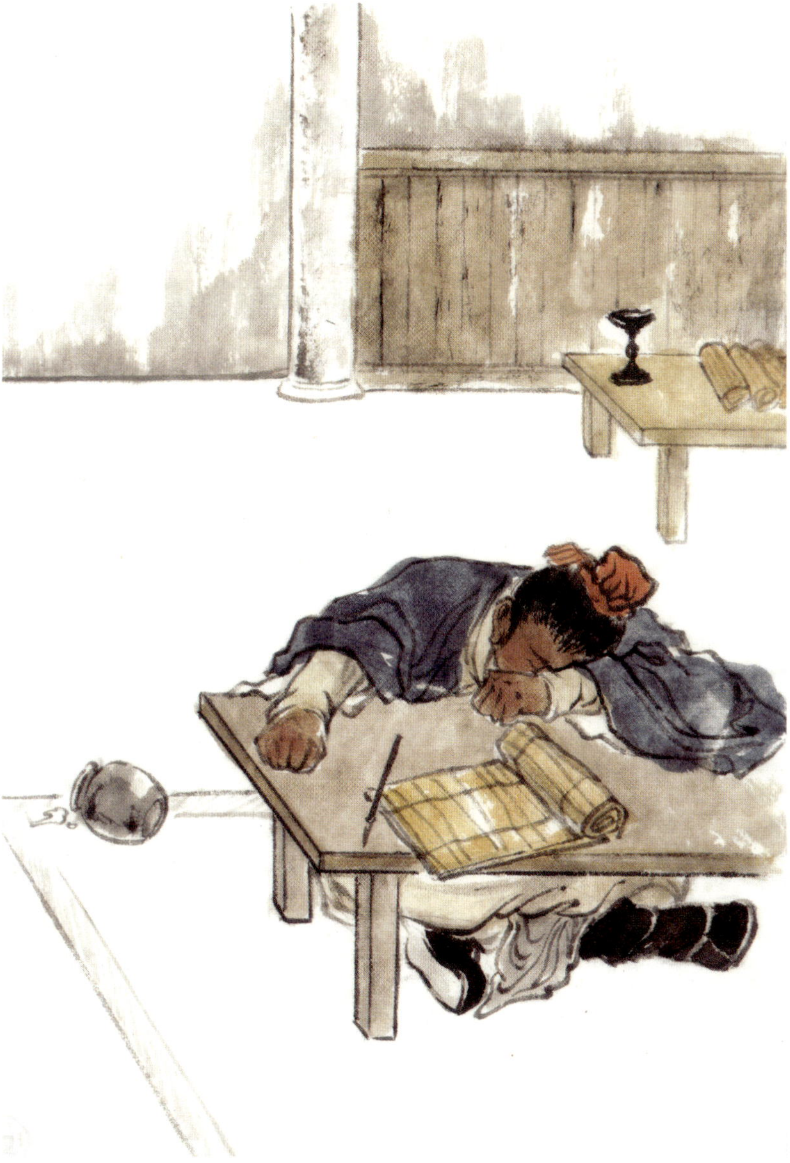

34.Rotten wood cannot be carved

【Source】

Zaiyu slept in broad daylight.

The master said, "Rotten wood cannot be carved and walls stained with excretion cannot be whitewashed. What's the use of blaming Zaiyu?"

The master said, "I used to listen to his words and believe his deeds would match his words, but from now on I will listen to his words and watch his deeds. It is because of Zaiyu that I have changed my idea."

The *Analects* ·Gongye Chang Chapter5.10

【Comments】

Confucius thought that daytime sleep was embodiment of laziness and thwarted people from working hard. Confucius did not want his disciples to be men of words but no deeds, so he severely criticized Zaiyu. Thanks to the strong warning, Zaiyu finally turned out to be one of the top disciples of Confucius, known for his industriousness and eloquence.

34. 朽木不可雕也

【原文】

宰予昼寝。子曰:"朽木不可雕也,粪土之墙不可杇也。于予与何诛?"子曰:"始吾于人也,听其言而信其行;今吾于人也,听其言而观其行。于予与改是。"

《论语·公冶长》5.10 章

【释文】

宰予在白天睡觉。孔子说:"腐烂的木头不能雕刻,满是粪土的墙壁不能粉刷。对于宰予,我还责备什么呢?"孔子又说:"以前我对人,听到他的话,便相信他的行为;今天,我对人,听到他的话,要考察他的行为。是因宰予而有这一改变的。"

【解析】

孔子认为大白天睡觉是懒惰,会使人志气松懈,不希望自己的弟子空有远大志向却不踏实行动,因而对宰予提出严厉批评。宰予终以好学深思,能言善辩,成为孔子的著名弟子。

老者安之，朋友信之，少者怀之
The elder are taken good care of and live in comfort,
friends trust each other and the young have good examples to follow

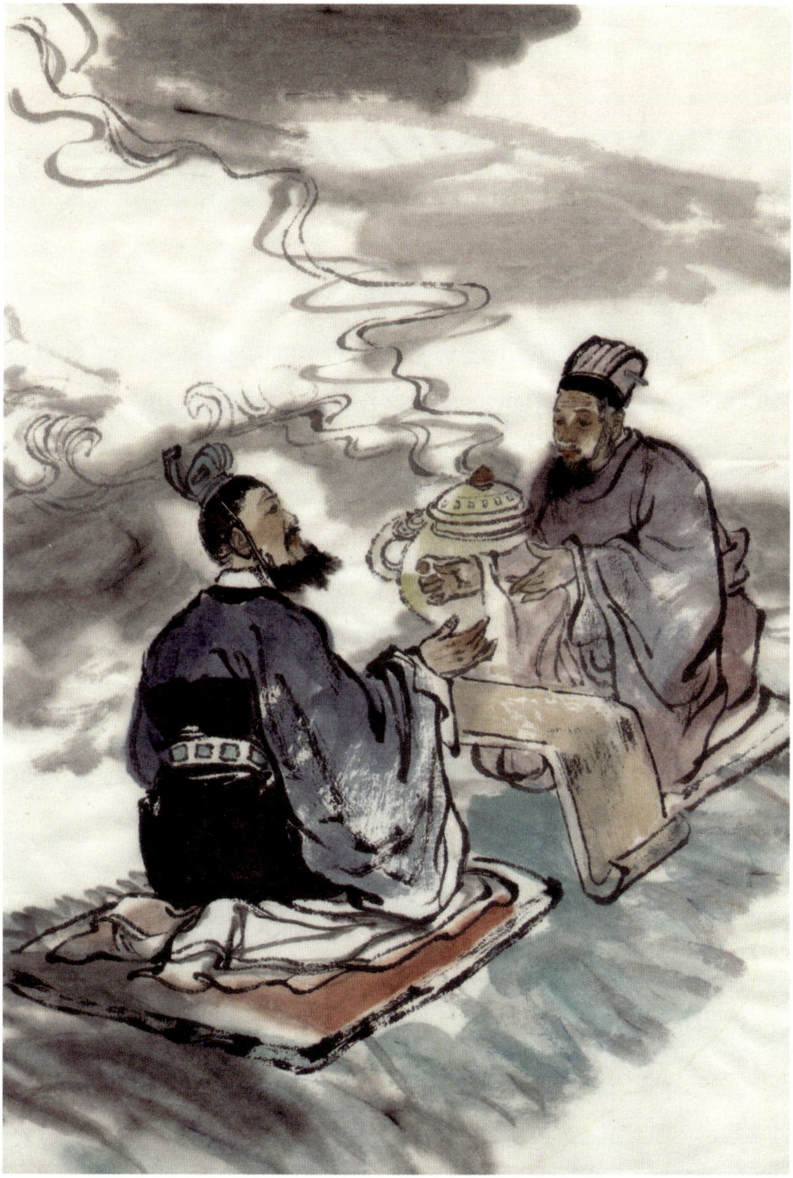

35. The elder are taken good care of and live in comfort, friends trust each other and the young have good examples to follow

【Source】

Yan Hui and Zilu were with the master.

The master asked, "What are your aspirations?"

Zilu said, "I would like to share my carriage, horses and clothes with my friends and feel no regrets or resentment if they are worn out."

Yan Hui said, "I would not brag of my ability or claim credit for myself."

Zilu asked the master, "Can you tell us about your aspiration?"

The master said, "I hope the elder are taken good care of and live in comfort, friends trust each other and the young have good examples to follow."

The *Analects* ·Gongye Chang Chapter5.26

【Comments】

Confucius encouraged his disciples to have noble aspirations. Zilu aspired to bring material benefits to his friends and Yan Hui hoped to enhance his moral cultivation. The aspiration of Confucius reflects the universal love of the humane.

35. 老者安之，朋友信之，少者怀之

【原文】

颜渊、季路侍。子曰："盍各言尔志？"子路曰："愿车马、衣轻裘，与朋友共，敝之而无憾。"颜渊曰"愿无伐善，无施劳。"子路曰："愿闻子之志。"子曰："老者安之，朋友信之，少者怀之。"

《论语·公冶长》5.26 章

【释文】

颜渊、季路两人陪在孔子身边。孔子说："何不各人说说自己的志向？"子路说："我愿意将自己的车马衣服与朋友共享，即使用坏，我也不遗憾和不满。"颜渊说："我希望不夸耀自己的好处，不表白自己的功劳。"子路向孔子说："希望听到您的志向。"孔子说："对老人，能使他们安逸；对朋友，能让他们信任我；对年轻人，能让他们怀念我。"

【解析】

孔子鼓励弟子立志，要求弟子志行高洁。子路之志重在物质上惠及朋友，颜渊之志重在精神上修养自己，孔子之志，则体现了仁者的博爱胸怀。

箪食瓢饮不改其乐

Remain cheerful with only a small bamboo basket
of rice to eat and a gourdful of water to drink

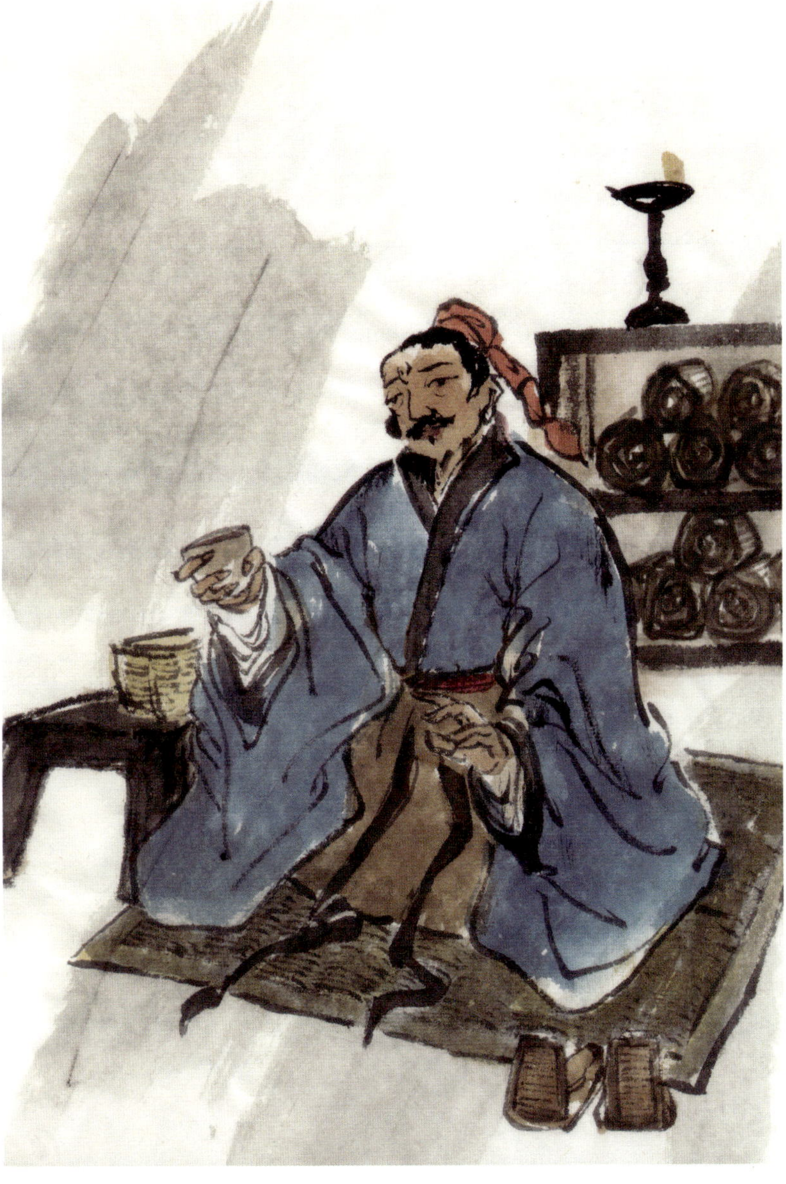

36. Remain cheerful with only a small bamboo basket of rice to eat and a gourdful of water to drink

【Source】

The master said, "Yan Hui is really the man with virtues. He has only a small bamboo basket of rice to eat and a gourdful of water to drink, a simple room in a shabby lane to live in. Other people cannot stand such destitution while Yan Hui remains cheerful in such poor condition. How virtuous Yan Hui is!"

The *Analects* ·Yong Ye Chapter6.11

【Comments】

It's not easy to be content to lead a poor but virtuous life. It's a basic requirement to the man of noble aspirations.

36. 箪食瓢饮不改其乐

【原文】

子曰:"贤哉,回也!一箪食,一瓢饮,在陋巷,人不堪其忧,回也不改其乐。贤哉,回也!"

《论语·雍也》6.11 章

【释文】

孔子说:"颜回真是贤啊!一竹筐饭,一瓢水,住在小巷子里,别人都受不了那穷苦的忧愁,颜回却不改变他自有的快乐。颜回真是贤啊!"

【解析】

安贫乐道是一个不容易达到和坚守的境界,但却是对一个有志之士的基本要求。

37. With perfect mix of simplicity and refinement, one can be called the man of noble character

【Source】

The master said, "When simplicity overweighs refinement, one seems rough. When refinement outstrips simplicity, one seems ostentatious. With perfect mix of simplicity and refinement, one can be called the man of noble character."

The Analects ·Yong Ye Chapter6.18

【Comments】

Simplicity refers to one's inner quality while refinement refers to outer appearance. The man of noble character possesses both good qualities and fine appearance.

37. 文质彬彬，然后君子

【原文】

子曰："质胜文则野，文胜质则史。文质彬彬，然后君子。"

《论语·雍也》6.18 章

【释文】

孔子说："朴实多于文采，就未免粗野；文采多于朴实，又未免虚浮。文采和朴实配合适当，才是个君子。"

【解析】

"质"指内在的品质，"文"指外在的仪容。既有美好的品质，又有美好的仪容，才算得上君子。

38. Liking it is better than understanding it while enjoying it is the best

【Source】

The master said, "Liking it is better than understanding it while enjoying it is the best."

The Analects ·Yong Ye Chapter6.20

【Comments】

Learning should be fun. Knowledge is not absorbed by being crammed into the brain. A learner should have a strong thirst for knowledge and enjoy learning.

38. 知之者不如好之者,好之者不如乐之者

【原文】

子曰:"知之者不如好之者,好之者不如乐之者。"

《论语·雍也》6.20 章

【释文】

孔子说:"懂得它的人不如喜爱它的人,喜爱它的人不如以它为乐的人。"

【解析】

学习不应是个苦差事,也不是把知识灌进大脑就行。人应该有发自内心的求知欲,喜爱学习,能从学习中获得快乐。

知者乐水，仁者乐山
The wise love water while the humane love mountains

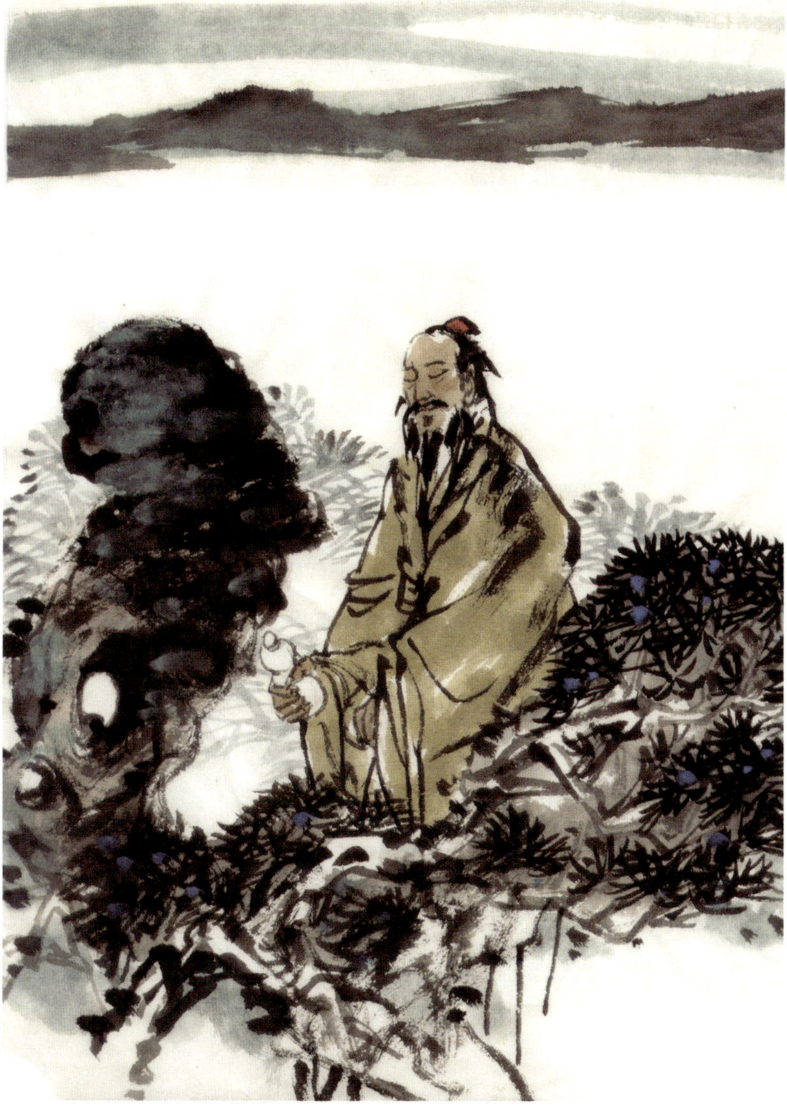

39. The wise love water while the humane love mountains

【Source】

The master said, "The wise love water while the humane love mountains. The wise love mobility while the humane love tranquility. The wise are cheerful while the humane live a long life."

The Analects ·Yong Ye Chapter6.23

【Comments】

Wisdom and humaneness are characters of two different kinds of people and they are emphasized varyingly on people and have correspondingly different external expressions.

39. 知者乐水，仁者乐山

【原文】

子曰："知者乐水，仁者乐山。知者动，仁者静。知者乐，仁者寿。"

《论语·雍也》6.23 章

【释文】

孔子说："聪明人喜爱水，仁人喜爱山。聪明人活动，仁人沉静。聪明人快乐，仁人长寿。"

【解析】

"智"和"仁"是人两类不同的品质，在具体的人身上各有侧重，因而有不同表现。

40. If you want to be established, help others be established. If you want to achieve success, help others achieve their success

【Source】

Zigong asked, "Suppose a person brings enormous benefits to his people and help them live a better life. What do you think of him? Is he a humane man?"

The master said, "He's more than a humane man. He's a sage. Even Yao and Shun could not achieve that end. Humaneness is that if you want to be established, help others be established. If you want to achieve success, help others achieve their success. If you treat others as you expect to be treated, you are approaching humaneness."

The *Analects* · Yong Ye Chapter 6.30

【Comments】

The supreme state of humanness is to seek benefits for all and help all live a comfortable life, which is also the lofty ideal of Confucianism. It's a high moral standard for a person to not only make progress himself, but also help others make progress. One can gradually achieve the goal by starting from things around him.

40. 己欲立而立人，己欲达而达人

【原文】

子贡曰："如有博施于民而能济众，何如？可谓仁乎？"子曰："何事于仁，必也圣乎！尧舜其犹病诸！夫仁者，己欲立而立人，己欲达而达人。能近取譬，可谓仁之方也已。"

《论语·雍也》6.30 章

【释文】

子贡说："假若有这么一个人，广泛地给人民以好处，又能帮助大家生活得很好，怎么样？可以说是仁道了吗？"孔子说："哪里仅是仁道！那一定是圣德了！尧舜都难以做到哩！仁道，就是自己想要站得住，同时也使别人站得住；自己想要事事行得通，同时也使别人事事行得通。能从身边选择例子一步步去做，可以说是实践仁道的方法了。"

【解析】

为天下民众谋利并帮助大家生活得好，是"仁"的最高境界，也是儒家的崇高理想。通过自己的努力，让别人跟自己一块进步，这是很高的道德标准，但可以从身边的事开始一步步去做，逐渐接近。

学而不厌，诲人不倦
Learn and never feel content. Teach tirelessly

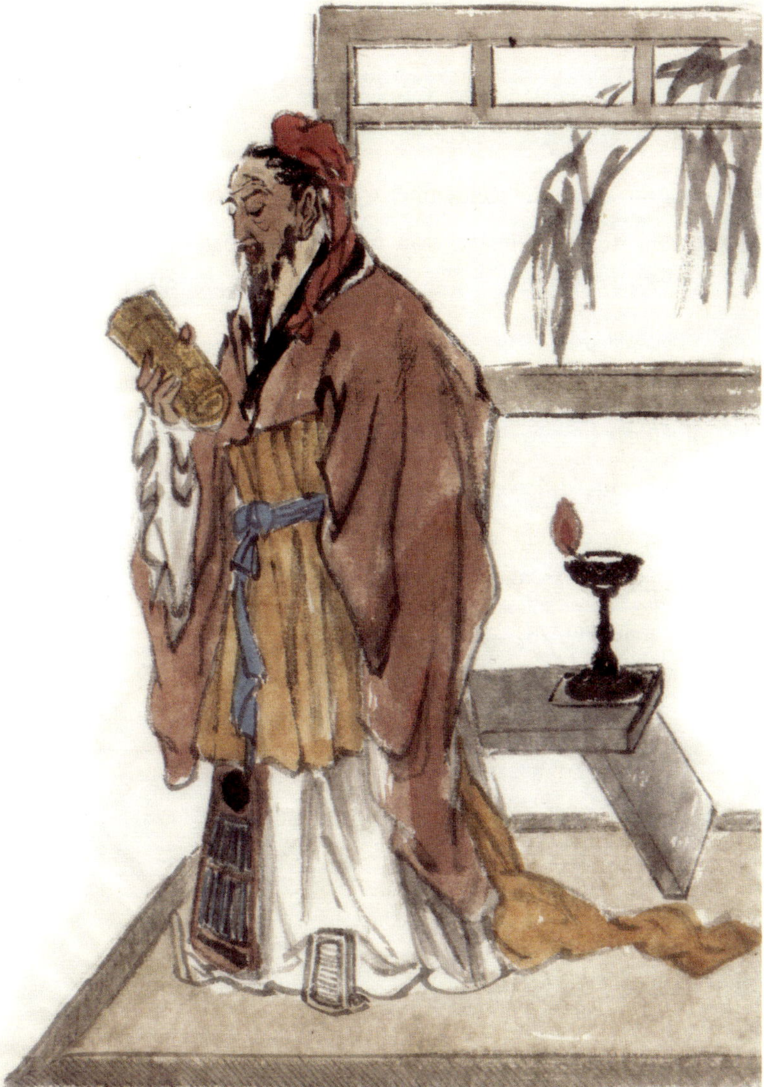

41. Learn and never feel content. Teach tirelessly

【Source】

The master said, "Remember what one has learnt. Learn and never feel content. Teach tirelessly. How many of the goals have I attained?"

The *Analects* ·Shu Er Chapter 7.2

【Comments】

Confucius did well in remembering what he learnt, learning without feeling content and teaching tirelessly, yet he thought he was far from attaining the abovementioned goals. It indicates that Confucius was a humble man and was eager to examine himself.

41. 学而不厌，诲人不倦

【原文】

子曰："默而识之，学而不厌，诲人不倦，何有于我哉？"

《论语·述而》7.2 章

【释文】

孔子说："默默地记住所学的知识，学习知识不觉得厌烦，教导别人不知道疲倦，这些事我做到了哪些呢？"

【解析】

本章所提的博闻强识、学而不厌、诲人不倦，孔子自身都做得很好，但他反问自己做到了什么，说明孔子很谦逊，有反省精神。

42.Draw inferences about other cases from one instance

【Source】

The master said, "Do not enlighten a student until he ponders the question but cannot figure it out. Do not enlighten a student until he wants to express his ideas but doesn't know how. I won't teach him if he cannot draw inferences about other cases from one instance."

The *Analects* ·Shu Er Chapter7.8

【Comments】

Confucius proposed enlightenment education. He advocated enlightening students on the basis of their independent thinking and asked them to draw inferences about other cases from one instance.

42. 举一反三

【原文】

子曰:"不愤不启,不悱不发。举一隅不以三隅反,则不复也。"

《论语·述而》7.8 章

【释文】

孔子说:"教导学生,不到他想弄明白而不得的时候,不去开导他;不到他想说出来却说不出来的时候,不去启发他。教给他一个方面的东西,他却不能由此而推知其他三个方面的东西,那就不再教他了。"

【解析】

孔子这里提出了"启发式教学"的思想,主张在学生充分独立思考的基础上再对他们进行启发、开导,要求学生能够自主学习、举一反三。

43. Follow my own inclinations

【Source】

The master said, "Wealth acquired by proper means can be gained. I'm willing to do inferior things like holding whips for officials to gain such wealth. Wealth acquired by improper means cannot be gained. In such a case, I'd rather follow my own inclinations."

The *Analects* ·Shu Er Chapter 7.12

【Comments】

Confucius was not against wealth and rank, but against wealth and rank acquired by improper means.

43. 从吾所好

【原文】

子曰:"富而可求也,虽执鞭之士,吾亦为之;如不可求,从吾所好。"

《论语·述而》7.12章

【释文】

孔子说:"财富如果合于道就可以去追求,即使是给人执鞭的下等差事,我也愿意去做;如果不合于道而不能追求,就按照我的喜好去做。"

【解析】

孔子不反对求取富与贵,但主张不能违背原则去追求富贵荣华。

不义而富且贵，于我如浮云
Wealth and rank achieved by improper means are like floating clouds

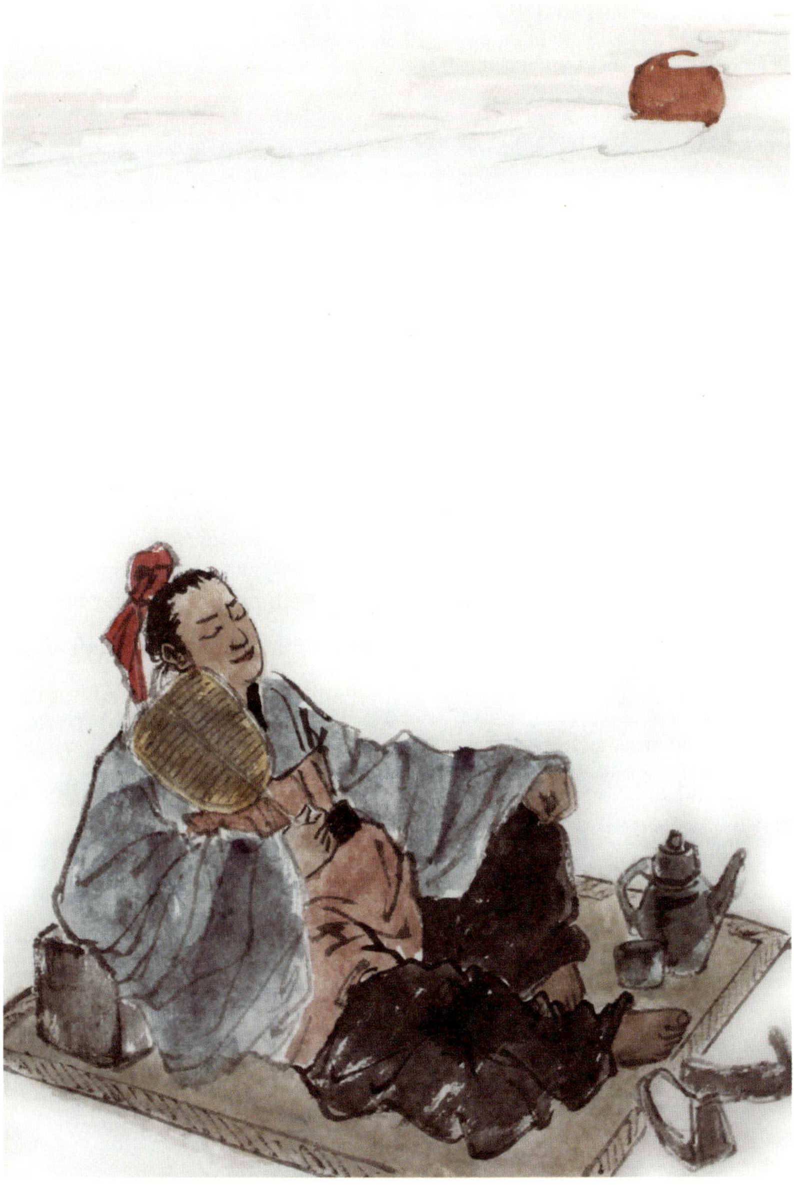

44. Wealth and rank achieved by improper means are like floating clouds

【 Source 】

The master said, "I can find pleasure in eating coarse grain, drinking plain water and sleeping with my elbow as a pillow. Wealth and rank achieved by improper means are like floating clouds."

The *Analects* ·Shu Er Chapter7.16

【 Comments 】

Confucius advocated being contented with poverty and caring only for the principles. He thought that the man of noble character should not pay too much attention to clothing, food and shelter. He pointed out that wealth and rank achieved by improper means were like floating clouds that could not stay long and men shouldn't try to retain possession of them.

44. 不义而富且贵，于我如浮云

【原文】

子曰："饭疏食，饮水，曲肱而枕之，乐亦在其中矣。不义而富且贵，于我如浮云。"

《论语·述而》7.16章

【释文】

孔子说："吃粗粮，喝白水，弯着胳膊当枕头，乐趣也就在这中间了。用不正当的手段得来的富贵，对我来讲就像天上的浮云一样。"

【解析】

孔子提倡安贫乐道，认为君子不应过于在乎自己的吃穿住。他同时提出，不符合于道的富贵荣华，如天上的浮云一般，无法留住，也不应企图留住。

三人行，必有我师焉
There is always someone for me to learn from

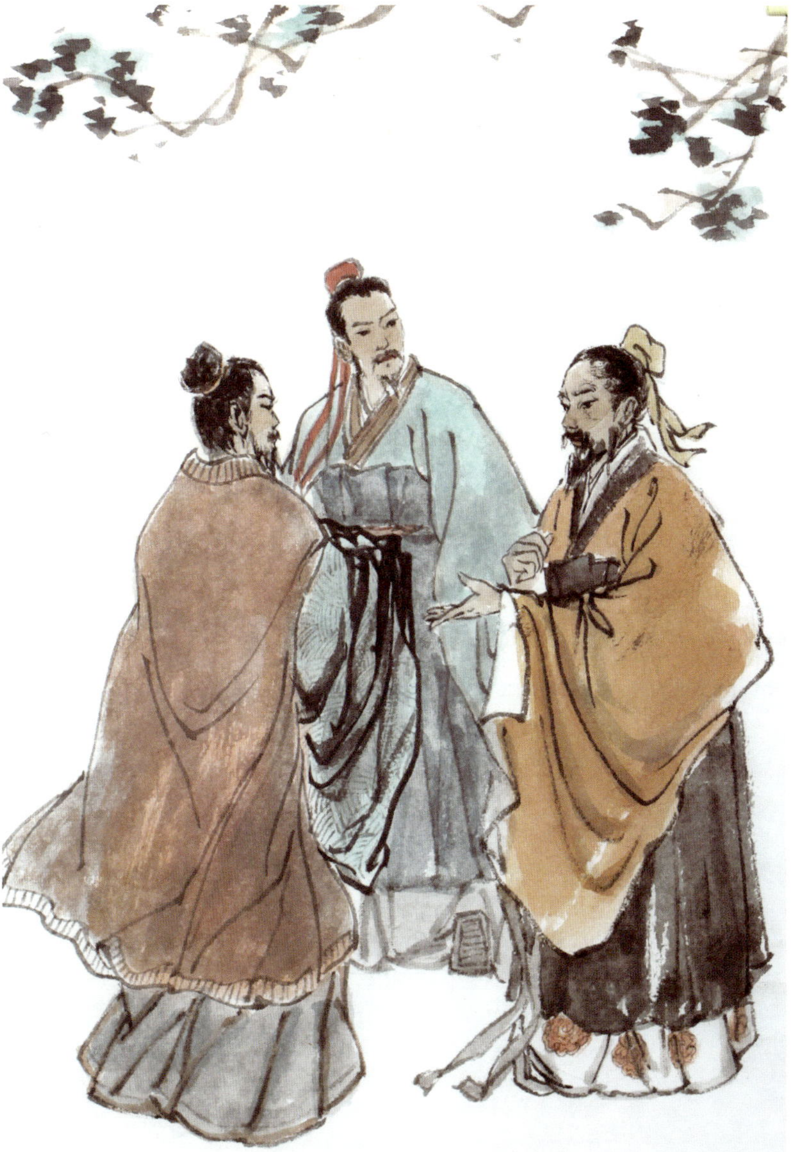

45. There is always someone for me to learn from

【Source】

The master said, "There is always someone for me to learn from. I shall learn from his merits to improve myself and take his shortcomings as a mirror to overcome my own."

The *Analects* ·Shu Er Chapter7.22

【Comments】

Each one has his merits and shortcomings. Confucius believed that one should be open-minded in learning and good at learning. One should not only learn from others' merits, but also take their shortcomings as reference to overcome his own.

45. 三人行，必有我师焉

【原文】

子曰："三人行，必有我师焉。择其善者而从之，其不善者而改之。"

《论语·述而》7.22 章

【释文】

孔子说："三个人一起走路，其中必定有人可以做我的老师。我选择他的优点学习，对他不足的地方引以为戒，改正自己。"

【解析】

人各有所长，亦各有不足。孔子主张虚心向他人学习，也应善于向他人学习，既学其优点，又以其不足为鉴戒。

46. If I want to achieve it, the humaneness will be at hand

【Source】

The master said, "Is humaneness far away from us? If I want to achieve it, the humaneness will be at hand."

The Analects ·Shu Er Chapter7.30

【Comments】

Humaneness is the human nature. Tireless efforts will help people achieve humaneness.

46. 我欲仁，斯仁至矣

【原文】

子曰："仁远乎哉？我欲仁，斯仁至矣。"

《论语·述而》7.30 章

【释文】

孔子说："仁难道离我们很远吗？只要我想达到仁，仁就来了。"

【解析】

仁是人天生的本性，经过不懈的努力，发挥主观能动性，就有可能达到仁。

士不可以不弘毅，任重而道远

A scholar should be unyielding for he shoulders a heavy responsibility and has a long way to go

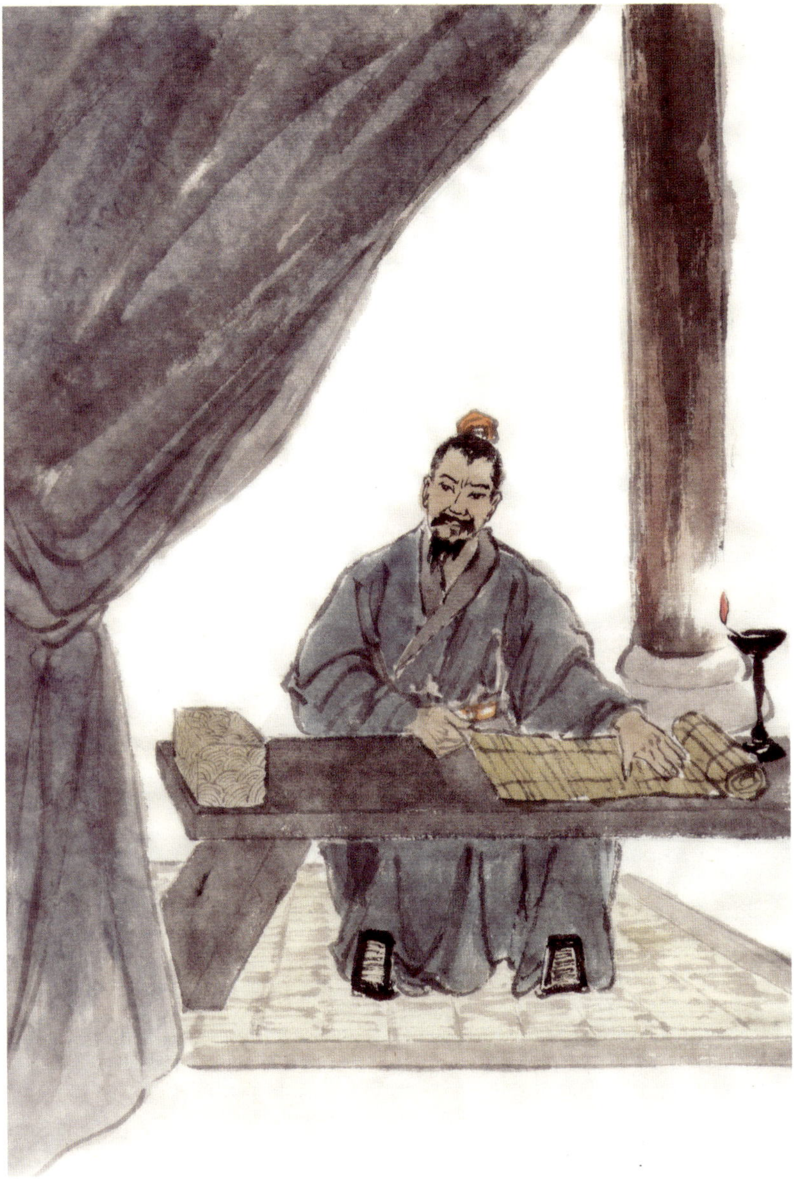

47. A scholar should be unyielding for he shoulders a heavy responsibility and has a long way to go

【Source】

Zengzi said, "A scholar should be unyielding for he shoulders a heavy responsibility and has a long way to go. Isn't it a heavy responsibility to achieve humaneness? Isn't it a long way to devote his whole life to the aim?"

The *Analects* ·Taibo Chapter8.7

【Comments】

To take the heavy responsibility and devote his whole life to it, one should be unyielding. What Zengzi said indicates the strong sense of historical mission and social responsibility and dedication of Confucianism.

47. 士不可以不弘毅，任重而道远

【原文】

曾子曰："士不可以不弘毅，任重而道远。仁以为己任，不亦重乎？死而后已，不亦远乎？"

《论语·泰伯》8.7 章

【释文】

曾子说："士不可以不刚强而有毅力，因为他责任重大，道路遥远。把实现仁作为自己的责任，难道还不重大吗？奋斗终生，死而后已，难道路程还不遥远吗？"

【解析】

责任重大，须要终生奋斗，就要求承担者具备刚强坚毅的品质。曾子的话表明儒家有强烈的历史使命感和高度的社会责任感，以及至死不渝的献身精神。

48.The *Book of Songs* inspires us

【Source】

The master said, "The *Book of Songs* inspires us. We are established in the society by acting in accordance with the rites and we improve our moral cultivation through music."

The *Analects* ·Taibo Chapter8.8

【Comments】

Confucianism believes that music is the token of the harmony of the universe. It edifies one's temper and purifies one's mind. The state of music is the supreme state of life and it stands for the accomplishment of one's moral cultivation.

48. 兴于《诗》

【原文】

子曰:"兴于《诗》,立于礼,成于乐。"

《论语·泰伯》8.8 章

【释文】

孔子说:"在《诗》里感发意志振奋精神,在礼上规范行为使自己立足于社会,在音乐中使自己的道德修养最终完成。"

【解析】

儒家认为,音乐表现天地万物的和谐,并能陶冶性情,净化心灵,音乐的境界是社会人生的最高境界,象征着人的道德修养的最终完成。

49. The master is free of the four defects

【Source】

The master is free of the four defects: speculation, arbitrariness, obstinacy, egocentrism.

The Analects ·Zi Han Chapter9.4

【Comments】

It's what his disciples thought of Confucius. Common people have the four faults, but Confucius did not. It's where Confucius's personality lied and why his disciples respected him.

49. 子绝四

【原文】

子绝四：毋意，毋必，毋固，毋我。

《论语·子罕》9.4 章

【释文】

孔子没有四种缺点：不凭空揣测，不主观武断，不固执己见，不自以为是。

【解析】

这是孔子身边弟子对孔子的评价。这四种缺点是一般人身上常见的，但孔子没有，可看出孔子人格之伟大和魅力之所在，也可以明白孔门弟子为何如此推崇和爱戴孔子。

叩其两端

Inquire about both pros and cons of the question

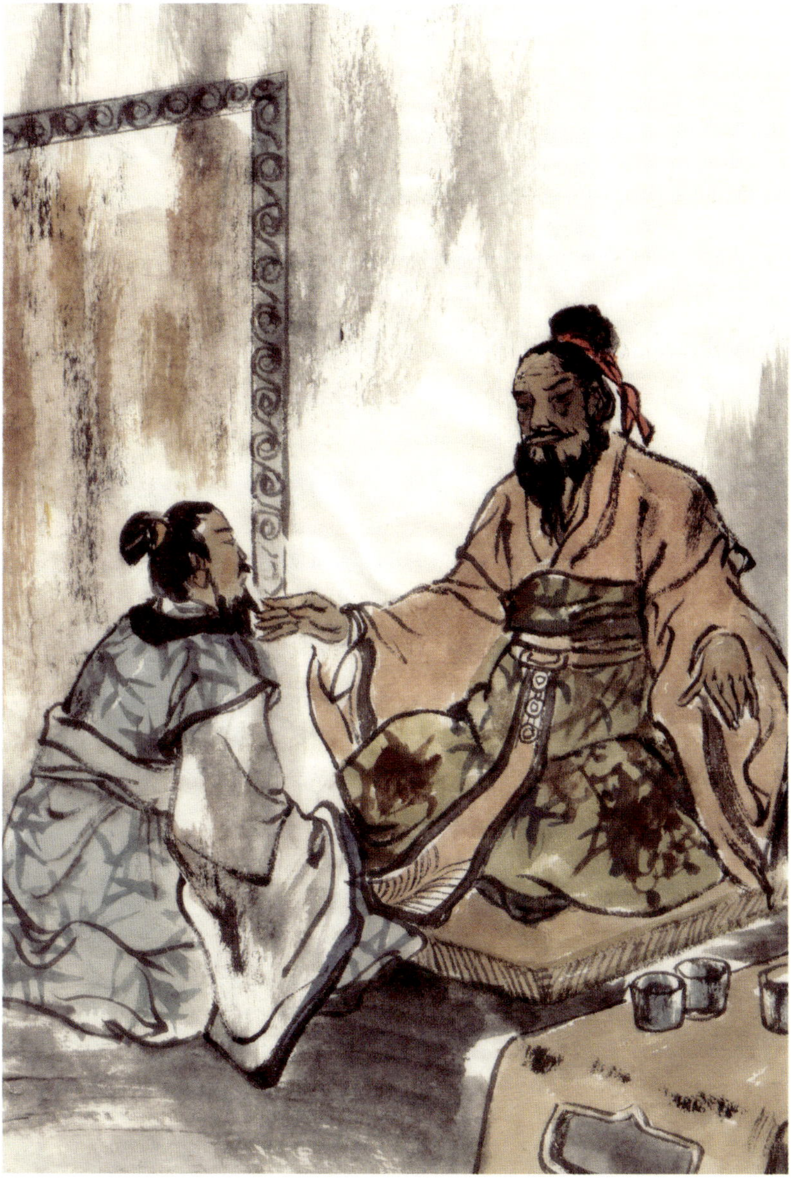

50.Inquire about both pros and cons of the question

【Source】

The master said, "Am I learned? No. A countryman asked me a question, but I didn't know the answer. I inquired about both pros and cons of the question and try to tell him the answer."

The Analects ·Zi Han Chapter9.8

【Comments】

Inquiry about both pros and cons of the question, like listening to both sides and choosing the middle course, is the most important way for Confucius to know things and solve problems. It emphasizes research and importance of getting an overall picture, based on which, one tries to find out right answers and solutions.

50. 叩其两端

【原文】

子曰："吾有知乎哉？无知也。有鄙夫问于我，空空如也，我叩其两端而竭焉。"

《论语·子罕》9.8 章

【释文】

孔子说："我很有知识吗？没有。有个乡里人来问我，我本来一点也不知道，我只是从他问题的首尾两头去盘问，问清方方面面的情况后，再尽量把正确的答案告诉他。"

【解析】

"叩其两端"和"执两用中"一样，是孔子认识事物和解决问题的最重要的思想方法和工作方法。其根本精神在于重视调查研究和掌握全面情况，并在此基础上找到正确的答案和解决问题的正确方法。

后生可畏
The young deserve to be treated with awe

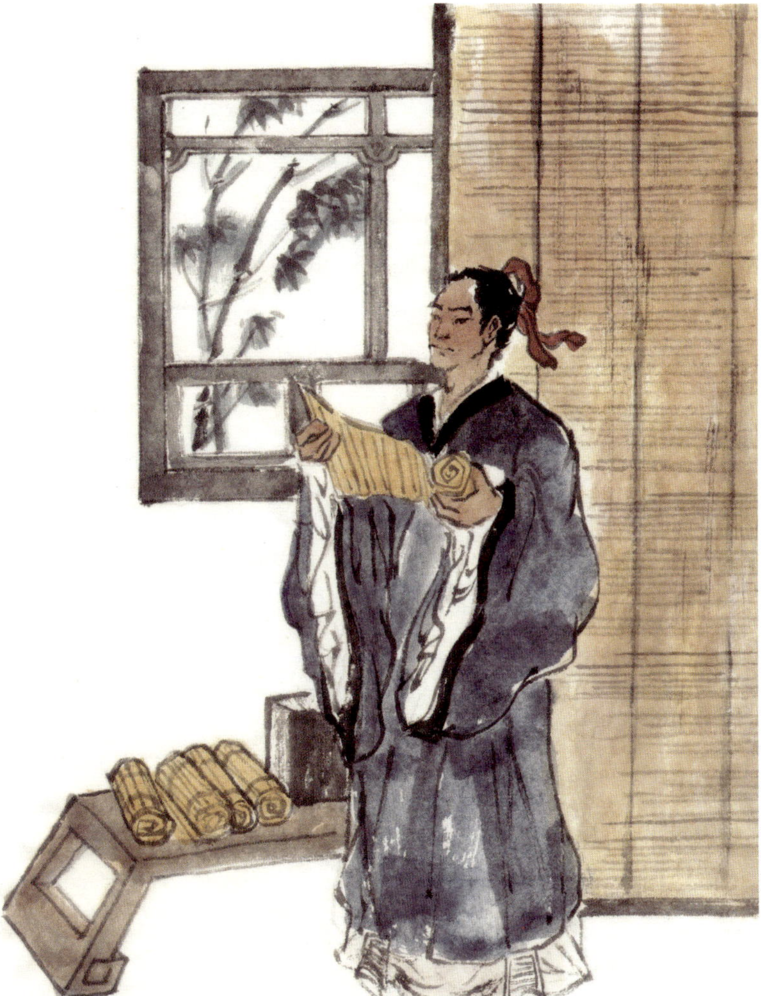

51.The young deserve to be treated with awe

【Source】

The master said, "The young deserve to be treated with awe. How do we know they will not be as good as this generation? Nevertheless, he who has not made his mark in his 40s and 50s has nothing to be awed."

The *Analects* ·Zi Han Chapter9.23

【Comments】

The young has time and energy and there are no limits to their promise. When a man is in his 40s and 50s, he has already spent half of his life and should have possessed admirable virtues and talents. If a man at this age accomplishes nothing, he will have nothing to be awed.

51. 后生可畏

【原文】

子曰:"后生可畏,焉知来者之不如今也?四十、五十而无闻焉,斯亦不足畏也已。"

《论语·子罕》9.23 章

【释文】

孔子说:"年轻人是值得敬畏,怎么知道他们不如现在的人呢?如果到了四五十岁还没有闻名于世,那就不值得敬畏了。"

【解析】

年轻人有时间和精力优势,前途无限。一个人到了四五十岁,人生过了大半,应当有一些值得人们尊敬的德行和才艺,如果还是碌碌无为、默默无闻,也就没有什么可让人敬畏的了。

52. A man will not be deprived of his aspirations

【Source】

The master said, "An army can be deprived of its commander in chief whereas a man will not be deprived of his aspirations."

The *Analects* ·Zi Han Chapter 9.26

【Comments】

The saying is very enlightening. We should be iron-willed and under no circumstances should we give in. When dealing with others, we should respect others' wishes and their personality and dignity.

52. 匹夫不可夺志

【原文】

子曰："三军可夺帅也，匹夫不可夺志也。"

《论语·子罕》9.26 章

【释文】

孔子说："一国的军队，可以战胜它，夺去它的主帅；一个普通的男子，却不能够强迫他，夺去他的意志。"

【解析】

孔子这句话对我们有很大启发：从自己方面说，要意志坚强，为了理想的实现，在任何情况下都不动摇、不屈服；从对待他人方面说，要尊重他人意志，尊重他人的人格和尊严。

岁寒，然后知松柏之后凋也

It's not until the weather turns extremely cold
can we see the leaves of pines and cypresses are the last to wither and fall

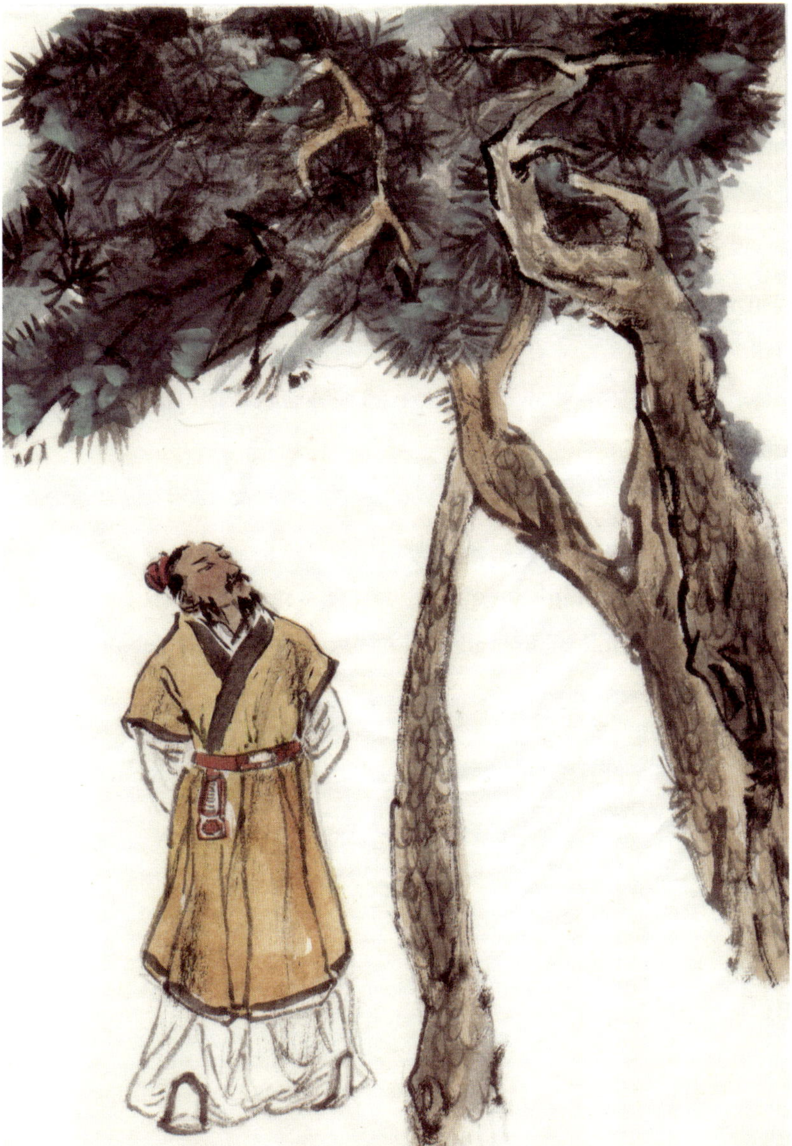

53. It's not until the weather turns extremely cold can we see the leaves of pines and cypresses are the last to wither and fall

【Source】

The master said, "It's not until the weather turns extremely cold can we see the leaves of pines and cypresses are the last to wither and fall."

The Analects ·Zi Han Chapter9.28

【Comments】

The saying highly commends the steadfastness of pines and cypresses. It's full of strength and has greatly inspired people through the ages.

53. 岁寒，然后知松柏之后凋也

【原文】

子曰："岁寒，然后知松柏之后凋也。"

《论语·子罕》9.28 章

【释文】

孔子说："季节转寒，才知道松柏是最后凋零的。"

【解析】

孔子这句话是赞美松柏的坚贞，充满无穷的意味和力量，激励古往今来无数人。

54. The wise have no puzzlement, the humane have no worries and the brave have no fears

【Source】

The master said, "The wise have no puzzlement, the humane have no worries and the brave have no fears."

The *Analects* ·Zi Han Chapter9.29

【Comments】

The wise knows morality and justice, so they are not perplexed. The humane are compassionate and they are always the first to bear hardships and the last to enjoy themselves, so they will not care about personal concerns. The brave are fearless and ready at all times to take up the cudgels for a just cause.

54. 知者不惑，仁者不忧，勇者不惧

【原文】

子曰："知者不惑，仁者不忧，勇者不惧。"

《论语·子罕》9.29 章

【释文】

孔子说："聪明的人不会被迷惑，有仁德的人没有忧虑，勇敢的人无所畏惧。"

【解析】

智者因为明了道义，所以能够不被迷惑；仁者悲天悯人，心怀天下，常能先天下之忧而忧，后天下之乐而乐，不会把个人的忧虑放在心上；勇者为道义无所畏惧，见义勇为。

厩焚问人

Ask about casualty after the stable caught a fire

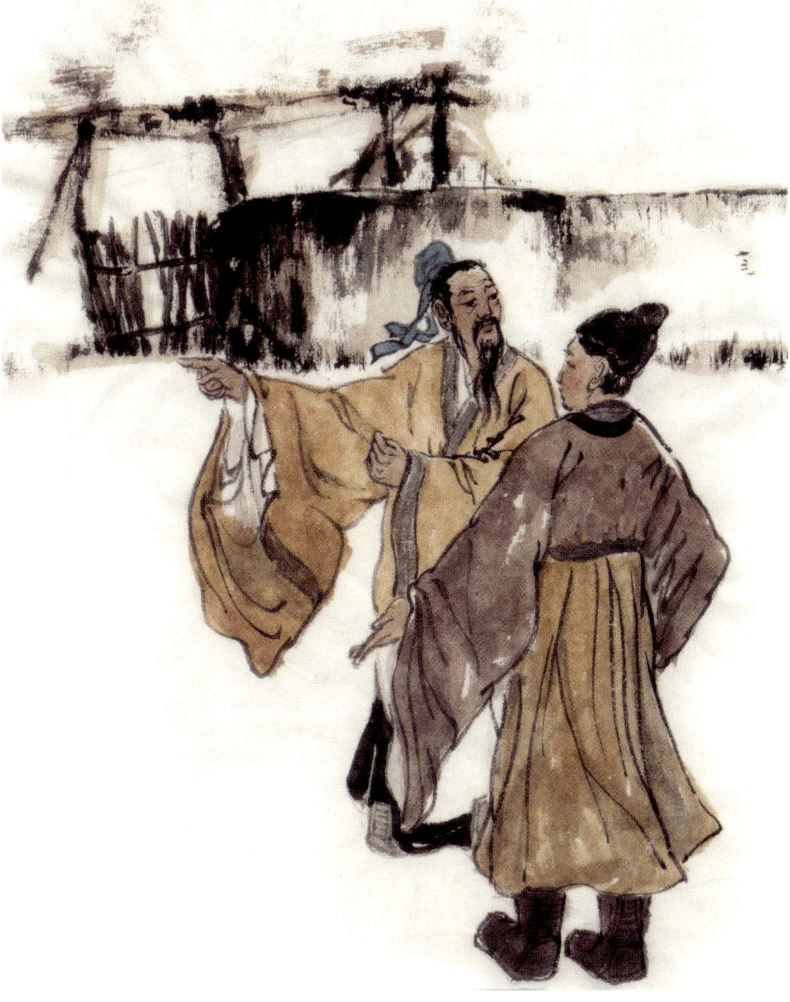

55. Ask about casualty after the stable caught a fire

【Source】

The stable caught a fire and was burned down. The master went home after having an audience with the sovereign and asked, "Is anyone hurt?" The master did not ask about horses.

The Analects ·Xiang Dang Chapter 10.12

【Comments】

Confucius asked about casualties after the accident, which indicated that he put people first and he was the man of great humanity.

55. 厩焚问人

【原文】

厩焚。子退朝,曰:"伤人乎?"不问马。

《论语·乡党》10.12 章

【释文】

马棚失火被烧掉了。孔子退朝回来,问:"伤到人了吗?"没有问马的情况怎么样。

【解析】

孔子听说发生事故后第一时间问人的情况,表明他把人放在第一位,表现了仁者的仁爱之心。

未知生，焉知死
We have not yet known life, how can we know death?

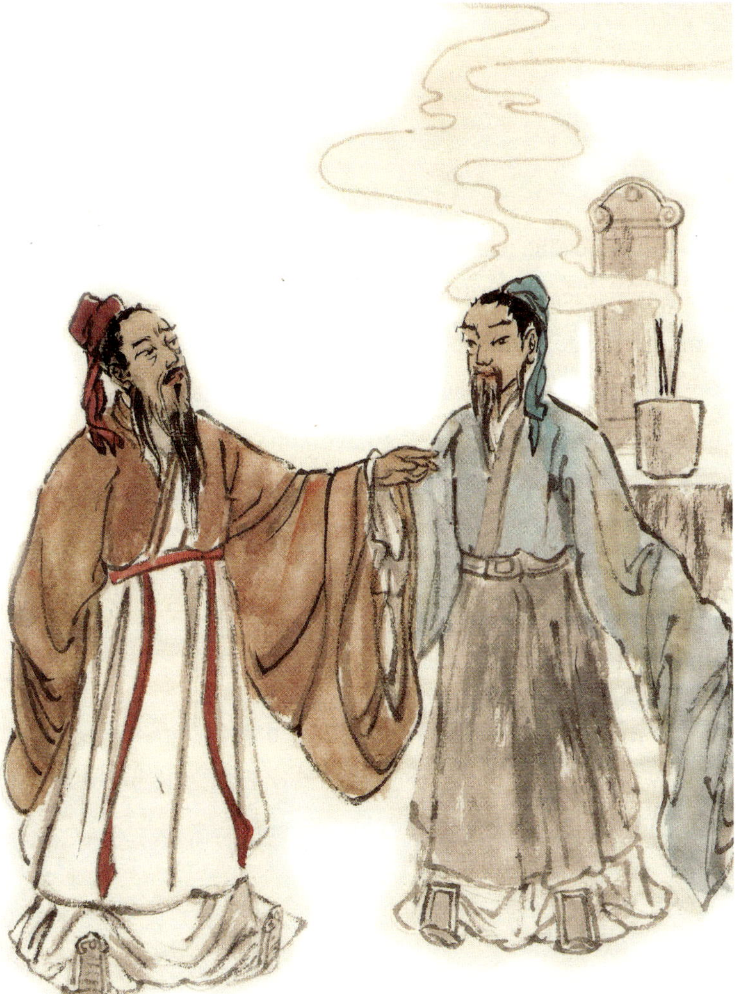

56. We have not yet known life, how can we know death?

【Source】

Zilu asked the master about how to serve gods and ghosts.

The master said, "If the living are not served, it's needless to talk about serving gods and ghosts."

Zilu asked again, "What will happen after death?"

Confucius answered, "We have not yet known life, how can we know death?"

The Analects ·Xian Jin Chapter11.12

【Comments】

Confucianism believes that life and death are two sides of one coin. When knowing life, men will know the world beyond death. So Confucius reminded Zilu to have his eye on life.

56. 未知生，焉知死

【原文】

季路问事鬼神。子曰："未能事人，焉能事鬼？"曰："敢问死。"曰："未知生，焉知死？"

《论语·先进》11.12 章

【释文】

子路问孔子如何奉事鬼神。孔子说："不能奉事人，哪能奉事鬼呀？"子路又说："那谈谈人死后的事吧。"孔子说："还没明白生，哪懂得死呀？"

【解析】

在儒家看来，死生本是一体，知道了人世间的道理，就可以推知鬼神世界的道理，故孔子此处提醒子路先处理好人事。

57. Discipline yourself and act in accordance with rites. It's humaneness

【Source】

Yan Hui asked the master about humaneness. The master said, "Discipline yourself and act in accordance with rites. It's humaneness. When every one does so, the whole society will become humane. It's entirely up to oneself to realize humaneness, not others." Yan Hui said, "May I know what a person should do to become humane?" The master answered, "Do not look at what is not in conformity with rites, do not listen to what is not in conformity with rites, do not say what is not in conformity with rites and do not do what is not in conformity with rites." Yan Hui said, "Fool as I am, I will do as what you have taught me."

The *Analects* ·Yan Yuan Chapter12.1

【Comments】

The kernel of rites is the ritual system, including the social system and code of conduct for individuals. Once the ritual system is disrupted, the society will collapse. Confucius believed that ritual system should be based upon humaneness. Humaneness is the inner basis of rites while rites is the external expression of humaneness. They are closely related to each other. Without rites, humaneness cannot be expressed while without humaneness, rites will be nothing but empty frame.

57. 克己复礼为仁

【原文】

颜渊问仁。子曰："克己复礼为仁。一日克己复礼，天下归仁焉。为仁由己，而由人乎哉？"颜渊曰："请问其目。"子曰："非礼勿视，非礼勿听，非礼勿言，非礼勿动。"颜渊曰："回虽不敏，请事斯语矣。"

《论语·颜渊》12.1 章

【释文】

颜渊问怎样做才是仁。孔子说："约束自己，照着礼去行事，这就是仁。一旦这样做了，天下都会趋向仁了。实行仁德，完全在于自己，难道在于别人吗？"颜渊说："请问实行仁的条目。"孔子说："不合于礼的不要看，不合于礼的不要听，不合于礼的不要说，不合于礼的不要做。"颜渊说："我虽然愚笨，也要照您的这些话去做。"

【解析】

"礼"的主要内容是"礼制"，是社会的制度秩序和人们的行为规范。制度受到破坏，社会就会崩溃。孔子认为，"礼制"应建立在"仁德"基础之上。仁是礼的内在依据，礼是仁的外在表现。没有礼，仁就无法显现；不依据于仁，礼将流于形式，二者紧密相连。

四海之内皆兄弟
All men under heaven are his brothers

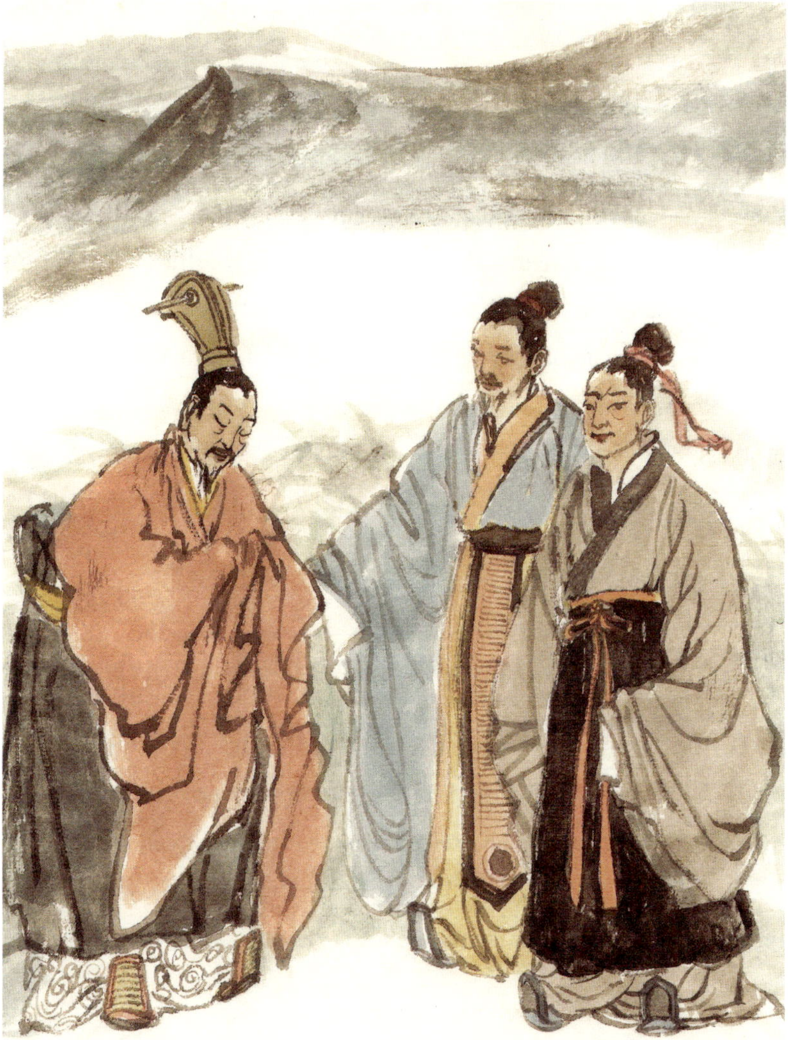

58.All men under heaven are his brothers

【Source】

　　Sima Niu said pensively, "Others have their brothers while I don't."

　　Zixia said, "I heard that life and death, wealth and rank are predetermined. The man of noble character does deeds carefully without making mistakes and treats others courteously. All men under heaven are his brothers. How can the man of noble character worry about having no brothers?"

The Analects ·Yan Yuan Chapter12.5

【Comments】

　　Sima Niu was separated from his brothers due to social upheaval. Zixia consoled him earnestly and greatly heartened him. Confucianism holds the belief that life and death, wealth and poverty are constrained by various social factors and they are not entirely up to an individual's subjective desire and action. Therefore, as long as men try their best, they should not care too much about the result. It's the Confucian life attitude.

58. 四海之内皆兄弟

【原文】

司马牛忧曰:"人皆有兄弟,我独亡。"子夏曰:"商闻之矣:死生有命,富贵在天。君子敬而无失,与人恭而有礼,四海之内,皆兄弟也。君子何患乎无兄弟也?"

《论语·颜渊》12.5 章

【释文】

司马牛忧愁地说:"别人都有兄弟,唯独我没有。"子夏说:"我曾听说过:死生有命,富贵在天。君子只要对所做的事情严肃认真,不出差错,对人恭敬而合乎礼的规定,那么天下到处都是自己的兄弟了。君子何愁没有兄弟呢?"

【解析】

司马牛的几个兄弟因为叛乱而离散,颠沛流离。子夏劝慰的话恳切而真挚,给人极大的安慰和鼓舞。儒家认为,个人的"死生"与"贫富",受个人与社会种种因素的制约,并不完全取决于个人的主观愿望和行为。因而,个人只要尽最大的努力去做就可以了,不要过分地在意或计较其结果。这就是儒家"尽人事而听天命"的生活态度。

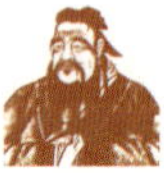

百姓不足，君孰与足

If the common people are wanting in money,
how can the sovereign have enough to spend?

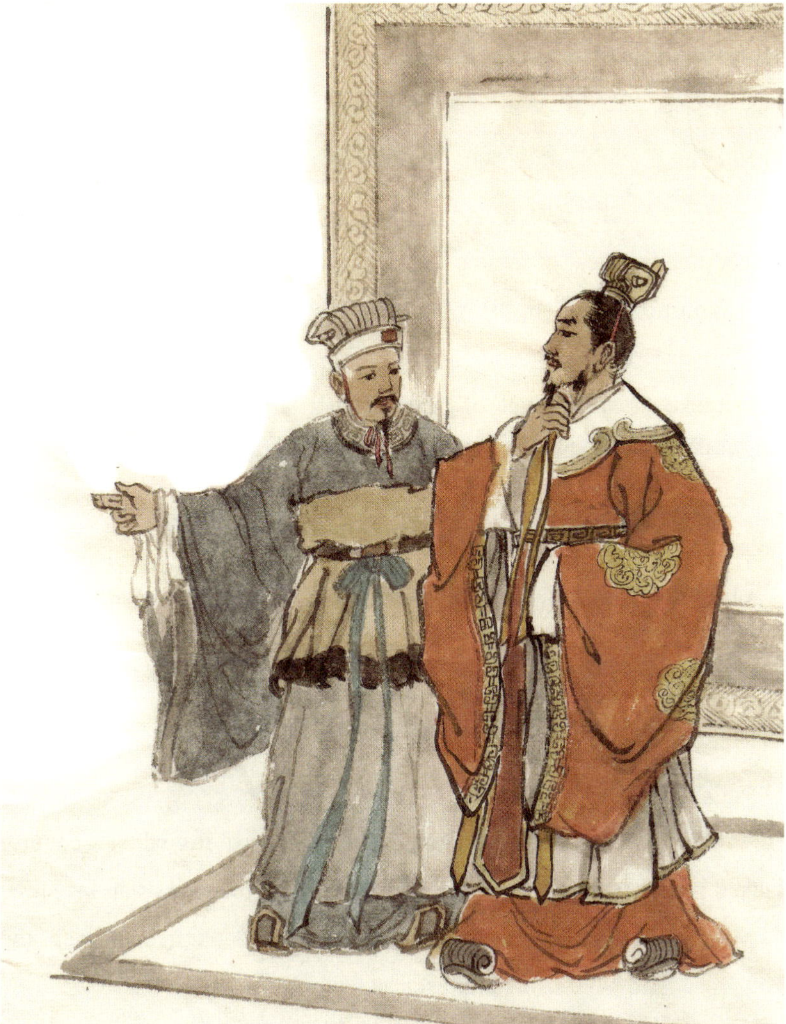

59. If the common people are wanting in money, how can the sovereign have enough to spend?

【Source】

Duke Ai of the State of Lu asked Youruo, "What measures should be adopted in a year of famine and extraordinary scarcity?"

Youruo answered, "Why not tax the common people one out of ten?"

Duke Ai of the State of Lu said, "It's far from enough to tax two out of ten, how can the tax of taking one out of ten work?"

Youruo answered, "If the common people have enough to spend, how can the sovereign run short of money? If the common people are wanting in money, how can the sovereign have enough to spend?"

The *Analects* ·Yan Yuan Chapter12.9

【Comments】

Youruo believed that it's not good to increase tax when a country lacked resources. On the contrary, tax should be reduced as an incentive to the common people and when the common people became rich, the country would have sufficient resources.

59. 百姓不足，君孰与足

【原文】

哀公问于有若曰："年饥，用不足，如之何？"有若对曰："盍彻乎？"曰："二，吾犹不足，如之何其彻也？"对曰："百姓足，君孰与不足？百姓不足，君孰与足？"

《论语·颜渊》12.9 章

【释文】

鲁哀公问有若说："遭了饥荒，国家用度困难，怎么办？"有若回答说："为什么不实行十分抽一的赋税呢？"哀公说："十分抽二都不够用，怎么能十分抽一呢？"有若说："如果百姓的用度够，您怎么会不够呢？如果百姓的用度不够，您怎么又会够呢？"

【解析】

有若认为国用不足时，增加赋税不是好办法，减少赋税舒缓和激励百姓，让百姓先富起来，国用自然会充足。

60. The ruler should behave like a ruler, the minister like a minister, the father like a father, and the son like a son

【Source】

Duke Jing of the State of Qi asked the master about how to govern a state.

The master said, "The ruler should behave like a ruler, the minister like a minister, the father like a father, and the son like a son."

Duke Jing of the State of Qi said, "Bravo. If the ruler doesn't behave like a ruler, the minister not like a minister, the father not like a father, and the son not like a son, I will have nothing to eat even though there's abundance of grain."

The Analects ·Yan Yuan Chapter12.11

【Comments】

Drastic social changes in the Spring and Autumn Period disrupted the hierarchical and name systems. The crimes of regicide and patricide were often committed, which in Confucius's opinion, was the main cause of social upheaval. So Confucius told Duke Jing of the State of Qi that "the ruler should behave like a ruler, the minister like a minister, the father like a father, and the son like a son". If so, hierarchies would be recovered, laying a solid foundation for the sovereign to run his country.

60. 君君，臣臣，父父，子子

【原文】

齐景公问政于孔子。孔子对曰："君君，臣臣，父父，子子。"公曰："善哉！信如君不君，臣不臣，父不父，子不子，虽有粟，吾得而食诸？"

《论语·颜渊》12.11 章

【释文】

齐景公问孔子如何治理国家。孔子说："做君主的要有君主的样子，做臣子的要有臣子的样子，做父亲的要有父亲的样子，做儿子的要有儿子的样子。"齐景公说："讲得好呀！如果君不像君，臣不像臣，父不像父，子不像子，虽然有粮食，我哪能吃得上呢？"

【解析】

春秋时期的社会变动，使当时的等级、名分制度受到破坏，弑君弑父之事屡有发生，孔子认为这是国家动乱的主要原因。所以他告诉齐景公，"君君、臣臣、父父、子子"，恢复这样的等级秩序，国家就可以得到治理。

君子成人之美

The man of noble character helps others achieve their virtuous purposes

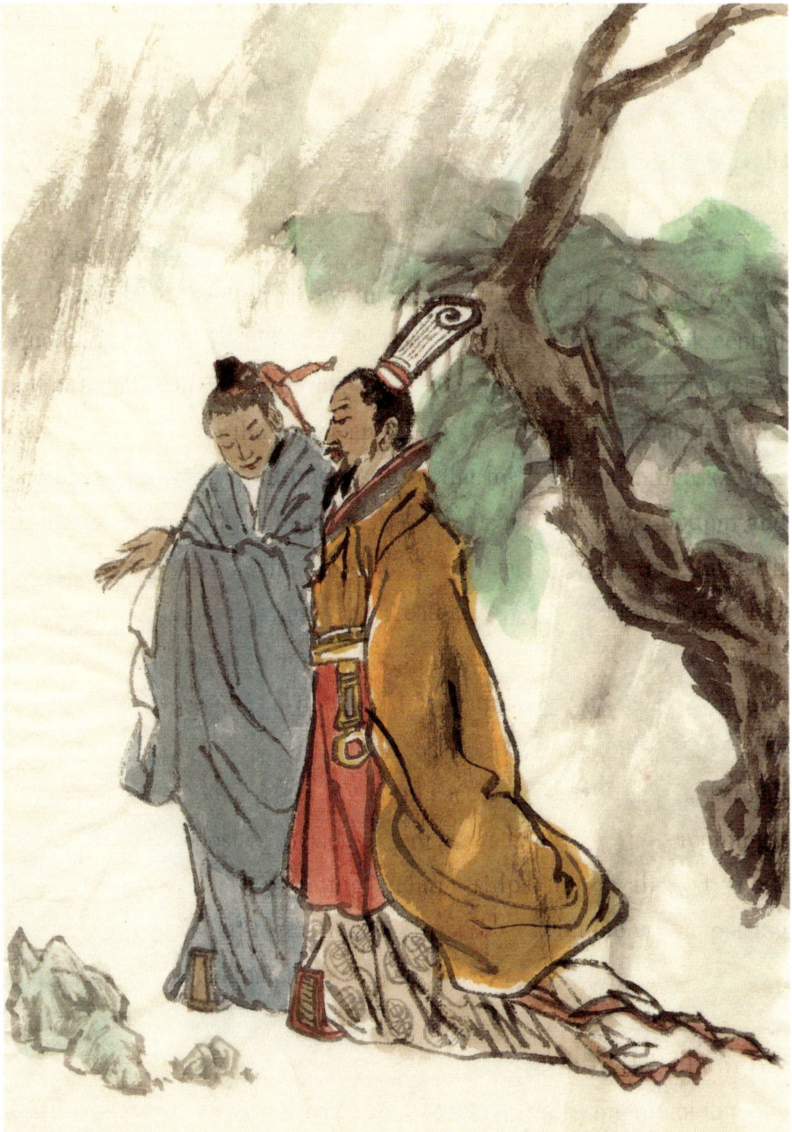

61. The man of noble character helps others achieve their virtuous purposes

【Source】

The master said, "The man of noble character helps others achieve their virtuous purposes and never helps them achieve their vicious purposes whereas the mean man does the opposite."

The Analects ·Yan Yuan Chapter12.16

【Comments】

One of the differences between the man of noble character and the mean man is to help others achieve their virtuous or vicious purposes.

61. 君子成人之美

【原文】

子曰:"君子成人之美,不成人之恶。小人反是。"

《论语·颜渊》12.16 章

【释文】

孔子说:"君子成全别人的好事,而不助长别人的罪恶。小人则与此相反。"

【解析】

君子与小人的区别之一,是助人为善还是为恶。

62.If you are an upright ruler, who else will not be upright?

【 Source 】

Ji Kangzi asked the master about how to rule a state.

The master said, "Ruling a state depends on uprightness. If you are an upright ruler, who else will not be upright?"

The *Analects* ·Yan Yuan Chapter12.17

【 Comments 】

Confucius stressed the importance of a good example set by political leaders. When subordinates don't do well, their superiors should be responsible for it. If the superiors conscientiously fulfill their duties, their subordinates will follow suit.

62. 子帅以正，孰敢不正

【原文】

季康子问政于孔子。孔子对曰："政者，正也。子帅以正，孰敢不正？"

《论语·颜渊》12.17 章

【释文】

季康子问孔子如何治理国家。孔子回答说："政就是正的意思。您本人带头走正道，那么还有谁敢不走正道呢？"

【解析】

孔子此处强调在上位者应起表率作用。在下位者做得不好，在上位者也有责任；在上位者若能尽职尽责，在下位者就会追随效仿。

苟子之不欲，虽赏之不窃

If you are not greedy for money, you will not see burglars
even though rewarding people for being burglars

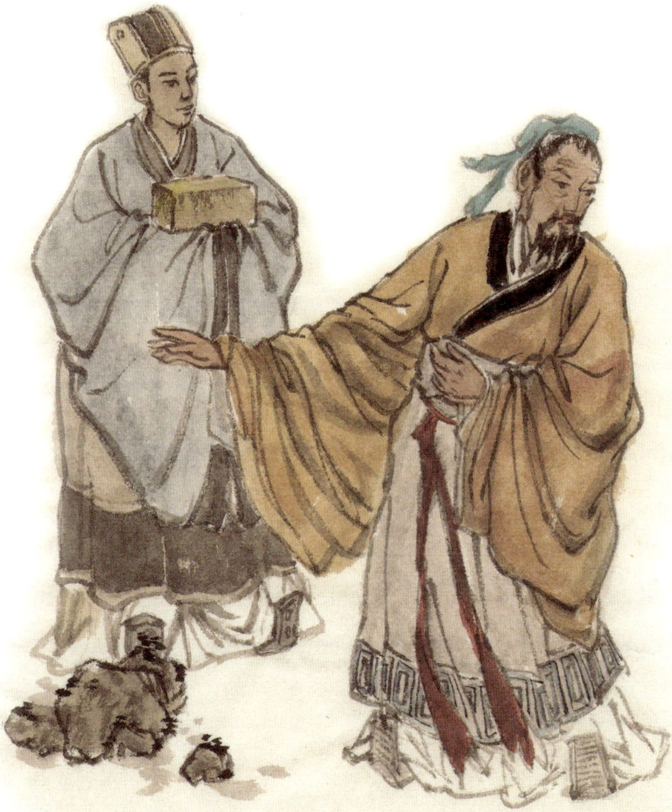

63. If you are not greedy for money, you will not see burglars even though rewarding people for being burglars

【Source】

Ji Kangzi worried about burglars in large numbers and asked the master for solution. The master said, "If you are not greedy for money, you will not see burglars even though rewarding people for being burglars."

The *Analects* ·Yan Yuan Chapter12.18

【Comments】

Rulers' exaction of money and other things from the common people will make life impossible for them. Consequently, common people will turn to burglary. The clan of Ji Kangzi rapaciously hoarded money, but expected the common people not to cause trouble. Confucius got right down to the heart of the problem.

63. 苟子之不欲，虽赏之不窃

【原文】

季康子患盗，问于孔子。孔子对曰："苟子之不欲，虽赏之不窃。"

《论语·颜渊》12.18 章

【释文】

季康子担忧盗贼为患，问孔子怎么办。孔子回答说："假如你自己不贪图财利，即使奖励偷盗，也没有人偷盗。"

【解析】

统治者搜刮民财、强取豪夺，必定弄得民不聊生、走投无路以致盗贼兴起。季康子家族在鲁国专权敛财，贪得无厌，却期待民众安分守己，孔子一针见血指出了问题的症结所在。

64. The humane love others

【Source】

Fan Chi asked the master about humaneness.

The master said, "Love others."

The *Analects* · Yan Yuan Chapter 12.22

【Comments】

Humaneness is to love others. First, humanness lies in filial piety and respects for elder brothers. A humane person loves his parents and siblings. Second, humaneness lies in loyalty and reciprocity. A humane person loves people around them and more broadly, he loves his country and his people and people around the world. It's the Confucian outlook on world and life and reflects the lofty ideal and broad mind of Confucianism.

64. 仁者爱人

【原文】

樊迟问仁。子曰:"爱人。"

《论语·颜渊》12.22 章

【释文】

樊迟问什么是仁。孔子说:"爱人。"

【解析】

"仁"就是爱他人。首先是讲"孝悌",爱父母和兄弟姐妹;其次是讲"忠恕",爱身边周围的人;再推广开来,就是爱国爱民,爱天下的老百姓。这是儒家的世界观、人生观,体现了儒家崇高的理想和博大的胸怀。

65. Set a good example and forgive the small mistakes of others and promote people with talents and virtues

【Source】

Zhonggong worked for the clan of Ji and asked the master about governance.

The master said, "Set a good example and forgive the small mistakes of others and promote people with talents and virtues."

The *Analects* ·Zilu Chapter13.2

【Comments】

Confucius believed that political leaders should set a good example for their subordinates to follow and promote people with talents and virtues to work at important positions.

65. 先有司，赦小过，举贤才

【原文】

仲弓为季氏宰，问政。子曰："先有司，赦小过，举贤才。"

《论语·子路》13.2 章

【释文】

仲弓做了季氏的家臣，问怎样管理政事。孔子说："身先士卒，赦免他人的小过错，选拔贤才来任职。"

【解析】

孔子认为从政为官者应为同僚、下属做表率，调动他们的积极性，举荐贤德有才能的人担任更重要的职务。

名不正，则言不顺
If the name is not correct, the words won't be justified

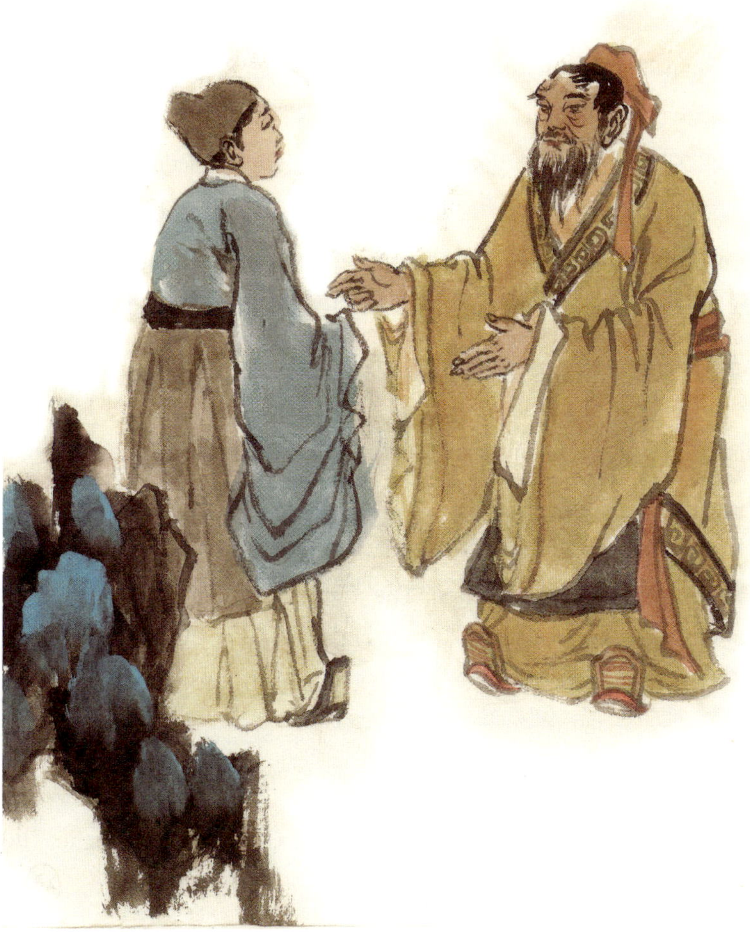

66. If the name is not correct, the words won't be justified

【Source】

Zilu asked, "If the ruler of the State of Wei asks you to be the chief minister, where will you start to do your duty?" The master said, "Rectify names." Zilu asked, "Do you have to do so? Isn't it pedantic? Why do you want to rectify names?" The master said, "How rude you are! The man of noble character will not offer an opinion on what they do not know. If the name is not correct, the words won't be justified. And if the words are not justified, nothing will be achieved. If nothing is achieved, rites and music will not prosper. If rites and music do not prosper, punishment will not be properly meted out. If punishment is not properly meted out, the common people will be at a loss. Therefore, the man of noble character will first rectify names and then express his opinions. What he says will lead to action. The man of noble character dares not speak or act in an incautious way."

The *Analects* ·Zilu Chapter13.3

【Comments】

Rectifying names is an integral part of Confucius's thought. The essence of it is to establish a hierarchical and orderly society for peace and stability, where people fulfill their own duties.

66. 名不正，则言不顺

【原文】

　　子路曰："卫君待子而为政，子将奚先？"子曰："必也正名乎！"子路曰"有是哉？子之迂也！奚其正？"子曰"野哉！由也。君子于其所不知，盖阙如也。名不正，则言不顺；言不顺，则事不成；事不成，则礼乐不兴；礼乐不兴，则刑罚不中；刑罚不中，则民无所措手足。故君子名之必可言也，言之必可行也。君子于其言，无所苟而已矣。"

《论语·子路》13.3 章

【释文】

　　子路说："卫国国君要您去治理国家，您打算从哪做起呢？"孔子说："首先必须正名分。"子路说："有这样做的吗？您太迂腐了！正名分干吗？"孔子说："仲由（子路的名）你真粗野！君子对于他所不知道的事情，总是存而不论。名分不正，说起话来就不顺当合理；说话不顺当合理，事情就办不成；事情办不成，礼乐也就不能兴盛；礼乐不能兴盛，刑罚的执行就不会得当；刑罚不得当，百姓就不知怎么办好。所以，君子定了名分就能够发表意见，说出来就能够行得通。君子对于自己的言论，是从不马虎对待的。"

【解析】

　　"正名"是孔子思想的重要内容，其实质是要建立一个等级分明、井然有序的秩序，从而各司其职，各尽其责，保持社会和谐稳定。

67. If the ruler acts properly, the common people will obey him without being ordered to

【Source】

The master said, "If the ruler acts properly, the common people will obey him without being ordered to. If the ruler does not act properly, the common people will not obey him even though being ordered to."

The *Analects* ·Zilu Chapter13.6

【Comments】

Officials should set a good example for the common people to follow.

67. 其身正，不令而行

【原文】

子曰："其身正，不令而行；其身不正，虽令不从。

《论语·子路》13.6 章

【释文】

孔子说："自身正了，即使不发布命令，老百姓也会去干；自身不正，即使发布命令，老百姓也不会服从。"

【解析】

从政为官者是否以身作则，影响其号令的施行，因为老百姓的眼睛是雪亮的。

富而后教
Educate people after they become rich

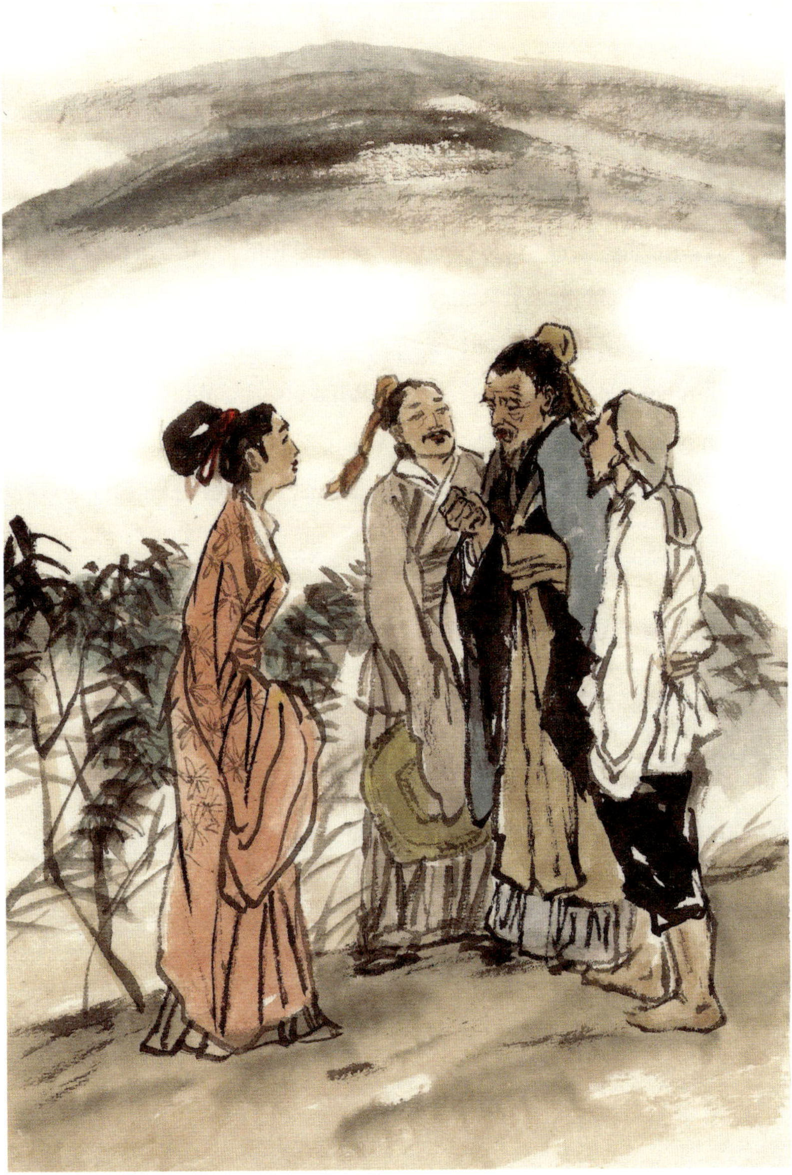

68. Educate people after they become rich

【Source】

The master went to the State of Wei and Ranyou drove the carriage for the master. The master said, "What a big population!" Ranyou asked, "What should be done to the big population?" The master answered, "Enrich them." Ranyou asked again, "What else should be done to them when they are rich?" The master answered, "Educate them."

The Analects ·Zilu Chapter13.9

【Comments】

Confucius put forward the idea of enriching and educating common people and he put prosperity before education. In the view of Confucius, enriching people is the most important and educating people is also important when they are rich.

68. 富而后教

【原文】

子适卫,冉有仆。子曰:"庶矣哉!"冉有曰:"既庶矣,又何加焉?"曰:"富之。"曰:"既富矣,又何加焉?"曰:"教之。"

《论语·子路》13.9 章

【释文】

孔子到卫国去,冉有为他驾车。孔子说:"人口真多呀!"冉有说:"人口已经够多了,还要再做什么呢?"孔子说:"使他们富起来。"冉有说:"富了以后又还要做些什么?"孔子说:"教化他们。"

【解析】

孔子此处提出"富民"和"教民"的思想,而且是"先富后教"。在孔子的观念中,"富民"是最重要的,而教化民众也十分重要,对富裕后的老百姓不能不施以教化。

欲速则不达
Speed hinders you from achieving goals

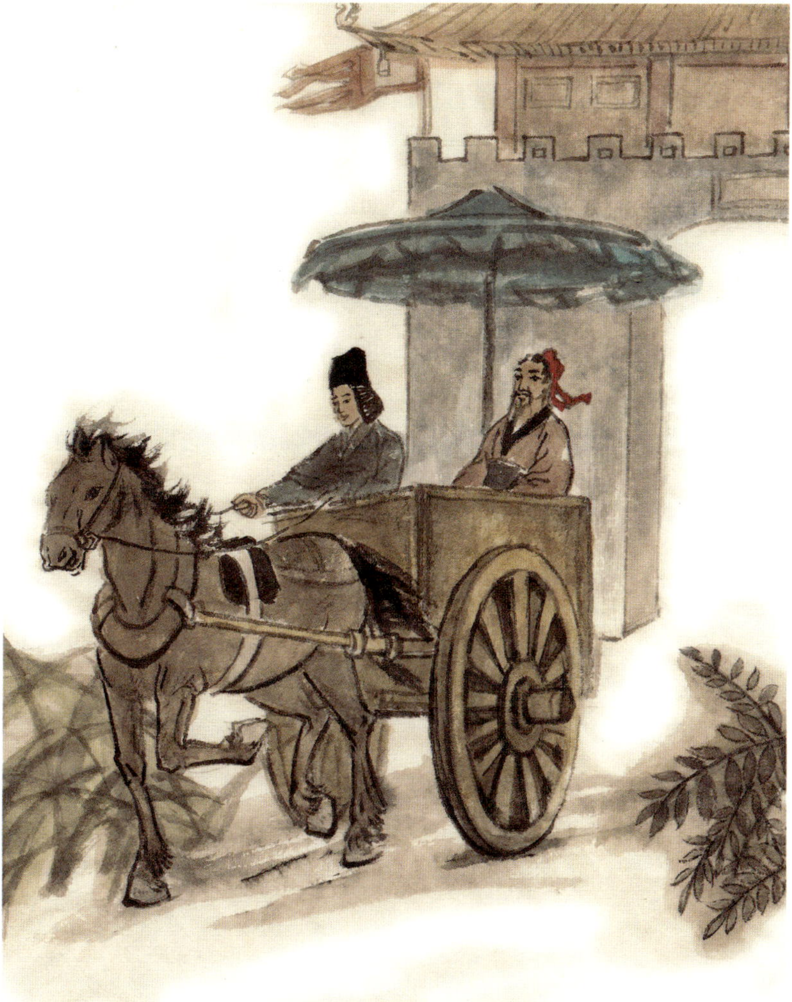

69.Speed hinders you from achieving goals

【Source】

Zixia worked as the house steward for Jufu and asked the master about governance.

The master said, "Do not pursue speed or small gains for speed hinders you from achieving goals and small gains prevent you from achieving great accomplishments."

The *Analects* ·Zilu Chapter13.17

【Comments】

Confucius asked Zixia not to seek quick success or instant benefits as an official. Otherwise, he could not achieve great accomplishments. It embodies dialectic opinion.

69. 欲速则不达

【原文】

　　子夏为莒父宰，问政。子曰："无欲速，无见小利。欲速则不达，见小利则大事不成。"

《论语·子路》13.17 章

【释文】

　　子夏做莒父的总管，问孔子怎样办理政事。孔子说："不要求快，不要贪求小利。求快反而达不到目的，贪求小利则做不成大事。"

【解析】

　　孔子要求子夏从政不要急功近利，否则就无法达到目的；不要贪求小利，否则就做不成大事，贯穿着辩证法思想。

70. Seek harmony rather than uniformity

【Source】

The master said, "The man of noble character seeks harmony rather than uniformity, while the mean man does the opposite."

The Analects ·Zilu Chapter13.23

【Comments】

"Harmony rather than uniformity" is an integral part of the thinking of Confucius. Harmony is achieved through respecting others and acknowledging differences. Uniformity is to efface differences by suppressing or flattering others. The difference between "harmony rather than uniformity" and "uniformity rather than harmony" is reflected in many facets and it indicates the profound philosophical thought of Confucius.

70. 和而不同

【原文】

子曰："君子和而不同，小人同而不和。"

《论语·子路》13.23 章

【释文】

孔子说："君子讲求协调和顺而不强行同一，小人只求强行同一而不讲求协调和顺。"

【解析】

"和而不同"是孔子思想的重要内容。所谓"和"，是指尊重他人，承认差异，从而协调致和；所谓"同"，是指压制他人或奉承他人，抹杀差异，强行同一。"和而不同"与"同而不和"的区别在许多问题上都有体现，显示出孔子思想的深刻哲理。

71. Fortitude, perseverance, artlessness and discreet are close to humaneness

【Source】

The master said, "Fortitude, perseverance, artlessness and discreet are close to humaneness."

The Analects ·Zilu Chapter13.27

【Comments】

Confucius believed that qualities like fortitude, perseverance, artlessness and discreet were in essence close to humaneness.

71. 刚毅木讷，近仁

【原文】

子曰："刚毅木讷，近仁。"

《论语·子路》13.27 章

【释文】

孔子说："刚强、坚毅、朴实、慎言，接近于仁。"

【解析】

孔子认为刚强、坚毅、朴实、慎言这些朴素、本真的品质接近于仁。

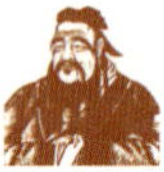

士而怀居，不足以为士矣

He who is reluctant to give up his comfort family life is unworthy of a scholar

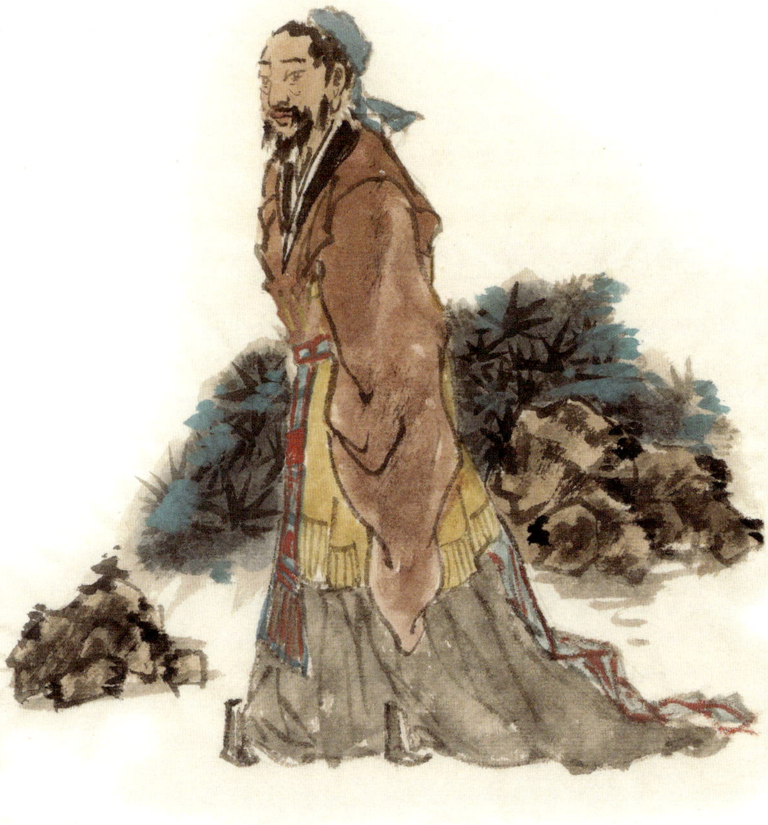

72. He who is reluctant to give up his comfort family life is unworthy of a scholar

【Source】

The master said, "He who is reluctant to give up his comfort family life is unworthy of a scholar."

The *Analects* ·Xian Wen Chapter14.2

【Comments】

A scholar should put the interests of his country and people above his family and comfortable life.

72. 士而怀居，不足以为士矣

【原文】

子曰："士而怀居，不足以为士矣。"

《论语·宪问》14.2 章

【释文】

孔子说："士如果留恋家庭的安逸生活，就不配做士了。"

【解析】

士应该以国家、百姓为重，留恋小家、贪图安逸不是士所应追求的。

73. The man of noble character is ashamed of too much talk but not enough action

【Source】

The master said, "The man of noble character is ashamed of too much talk but not enough action."

The *Analects* ·Xian Wen Chapter14.27

【Comments】

In Confucius' opinion, people should speak little but do much, not vice versa.

73. 君子耻其言而过其行

【原文】

子曰:"君子耻其言而过其行。"

《论语·宪问》14.27 章

【释文】

孔子说:"君子以说得多而做得少为耻。"

【解析】

孔子希望人们少说多做,而不要只说不做或多说少做。

知其不可而为之
Knowing it's of no use, but keeping on doing it

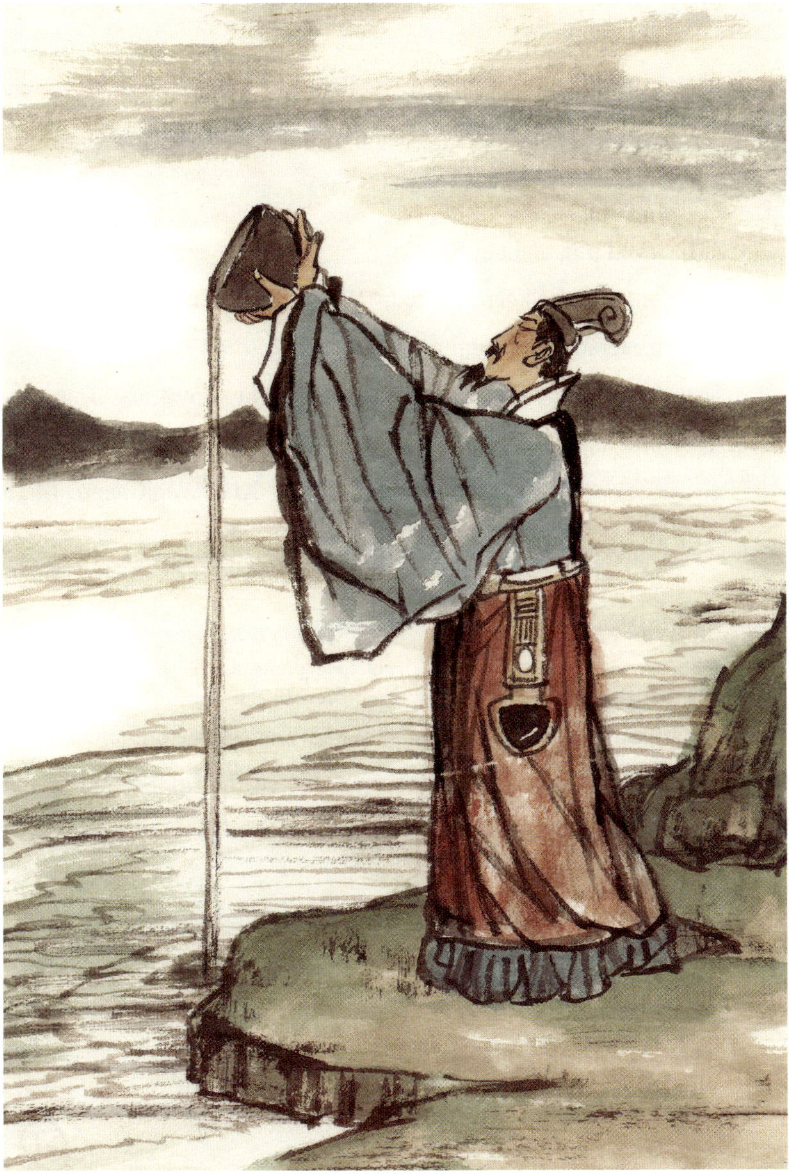

74. Knowing it's of no use, but keeping on doing it

【Source】

　　Zilu stayed one night at Shimen.

　　At dawn, the gate keeper asked, "Where are you from?"

　　Zilu answered, "I'm from the master Kong's house."

　　The gate keeper said, "Isn't he the man who knows it's of no use, but keeps on doing it?"

The Analects ·Xian Wen Chapter14.38

【Comments】

　　Successes come from hard struggle. Knowing it's of no use, but keeping on doing it is a testament of perseverance of Confucius. What the gate keeper said about Confucius reflected the impression of the common people of his own generation on Confucius.

74. 知其不可而为之

【原文】

子路宿于石门。晨门曰:"奚自?"子路曰:"自孔氏。"曰:"是知其不可而为之者与?"

《论语·宪问》14.38 章

【释文】

子路在石门住了一宿。早晨看门的人问:"从哪里来?"子路说:"从孔子那里来。"看门的人说:"是那个明知做不到却还要去做的人吗?"

【解析】

许多成功要经过艰苦奋斗得来,孔子"知其不可而为之",反映出他孜孜不倦、锲而不舍的执着精神。从这位看门人的话中,也可以见出当时普通人对孔子的评论。

75.Cultivate yourself and make the common people live in happiness and peace

【 Source 】

　　Zilu asked the master about how to be the man of noble character.

　　The master said, "Cultivate yourself and keep a respectful attitude."

　　Zilu asked, "Is it enough?"

　　The master answered, "Cultivate yourself and make the common people live in happiness and peace. Even Yao and Shun could not achieve the two aims."

The Analects ·Xian Wen Chapter14.42

【 Comments 】

　　Confucius discussed how to be the man of noble character with his disciple through questions and answers. Confucius thought that the man of noble character should cultivate himself first and more importantly, let common people live in happiness and peace.

75. 修己以安百姓

【原文】

子路问君子。子曰:"修己以敬。"曰:"如斯而已乎?"曰:"修己以安人。"曰:"如斯而已乎?"曰:"修己以安百姓。修己以安百姓,尧舜其犹病诸!"

《论语·宪问》14.42 章

【释文】

子路问如何做君子。孔子说:"修养自己,保持严肃恭敬的态度。"子路说:"这样就够了吗?"孔子说:"修养自己,使周围的人们安乐。"子路说:"这样就够了吗?"孔子说:"修养自己,使所有百姓都安乐。修养自己使所有百姓都安乐,尧舜还怕难于做到呢!"

【解析】

孔子这里再谈如何成为君子,弟子逐层追问,孔子就逐层解答。孔子认为,君子首先要修养好自己,更重要的是让周边的人、全天下的百姓安乐。

君子固穷
When in destitution, the man of noble character
will preserve his moral integrity

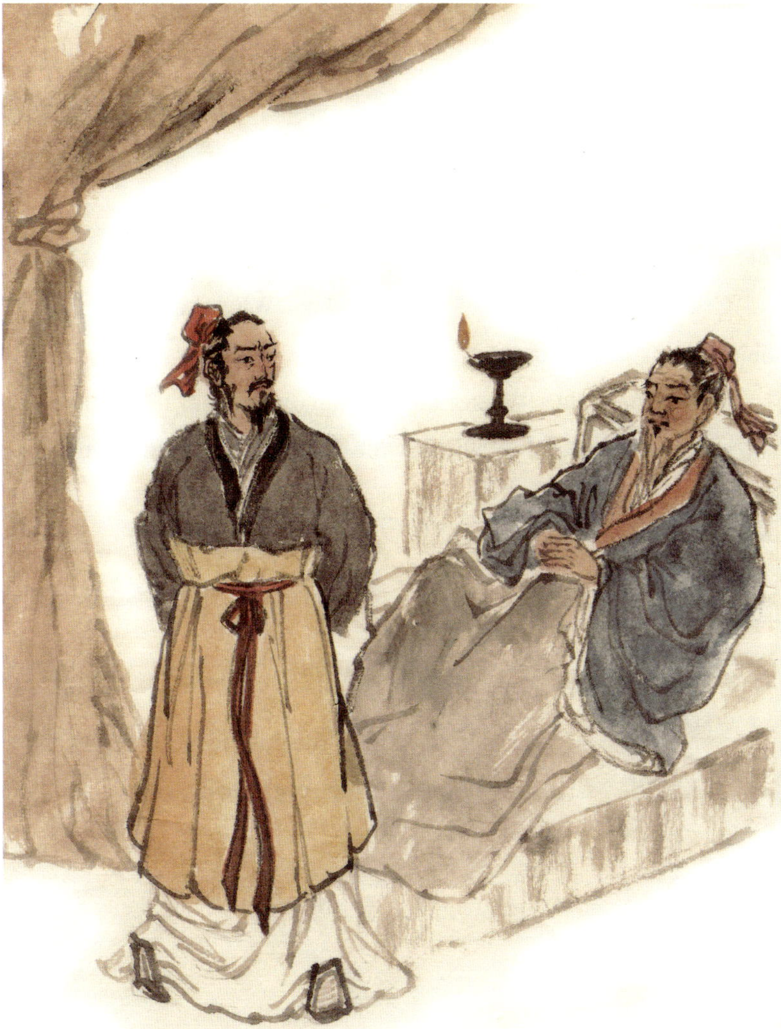

76. When in destitution, the man of noble character will preserve his moral integrity

【Source】

Confucius and his disciples ran out of food supply at the State of Chen. All the attendants were dispirited.

Zilu was angry and asked the master, "Why should the man of noble character suffer destitution?"

The master said, "When in destitution, the man of noble character will preserve his moral integrity while the mean man will commit all manner of evil."

The *Analects* ·Wei Ling Gong Chapter15.2

【Comments】

Sturdy grass withstands high winds; true gold stands the test of fire. Adversity is the best testing ground for moral stamina.

76. 君子固穷

【原文】

在陈绝粮,从者病,莫能兴。子路愠见曰:"君子亦有穷乎?"子曰:"君子固穷,小人穷斯滥矣。"

《论语·卫灵公》15.2 章

【释文】

孔子和随行弟子在陈断了粮食,随从的人都疲困不堪,没有人能振作起来。子路怒气冲冲地来见孔子,说:"君子也有穷困的时候吗?"孔子说:"君子在穷困时仍能固守自己的节操,小人穷困时就毫无节制地胡作非为了。"

【解析】

疾风知劲草,烈火见真金,在艰苦危难之时,才更能看清一个人的品德节操。

杀身成仁

Sacrifice his life for humaneness

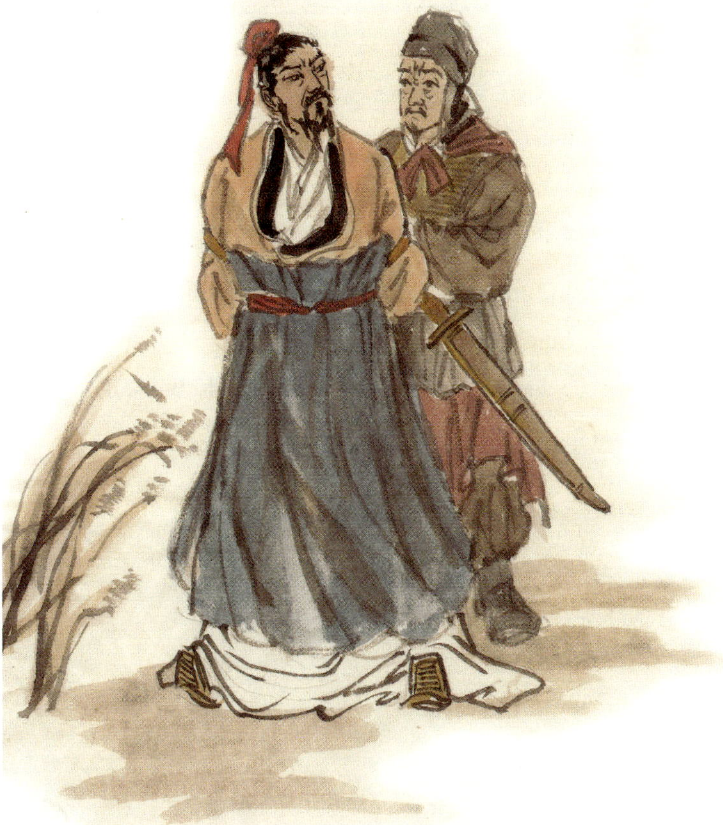

77.Sacrifice his life for humaneness

【Source】

The master said, "The man with lofty ideals will never sacrifice humaneness for his life, but prefer to sacrifice his life for humaneness."

The *Analects* ·Wei Ling Gong Chapter15.9

【Comments】

"Sacrifice his life for humaneness" means that one stands ready to die for the sake of humaneness. It's the integrity of the man with lofty ideals. Without it, he doesn't live up to the man with lofty ideals.

77. 杀身成仁

【原文】

子曰:"志士仁人,无求生以害仁,有杀身以成仁。"

《论语·卫灵公》15.9 章

【释文】

孔子说:"志士仁人,没有贪生怕死而损害仁的,只有牺牲自己的性命来成全仁的。"

【解析】

"杀身成仁",就是在生死关头宁可舍弃自己的生命也要保全"仁"。这是志士仁人的气节,缺少这样的气节,就不配称志士仁人。

工欲善其事，必先利其器
A craftsman must sharpen his tools first if he is to do his work well

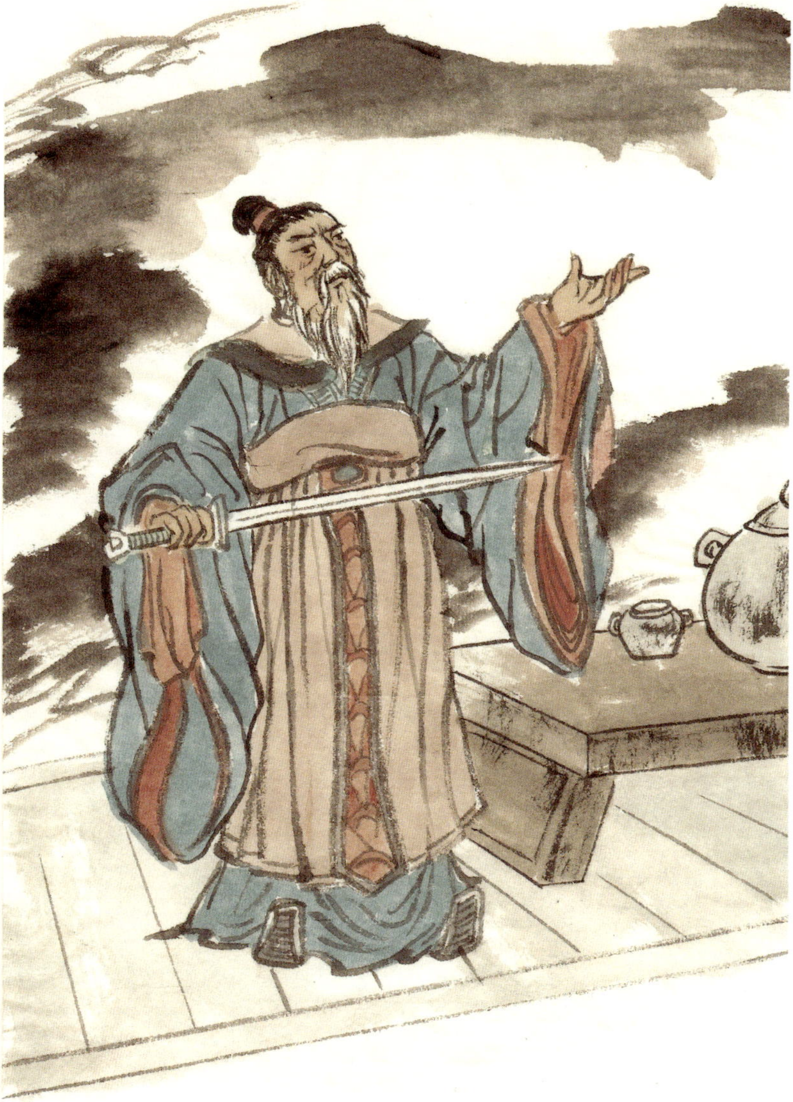

78. A craftsman must sharpen his tools first if he is to do his work well

【Source】

Zigong asked the master about humaneness.

The master said, "A craftsman must sharpen his tools first if he is to do his work well. Living in the state, you should serve the officials with virtues and make friends with scholars with humaneness."

The Analects ·Wei Ling Gong Chapter15.10

【Comments】

Confucius used the saying "a craftsman must sharpen his tools first if he is to do his work well" as an analogy. He explained that one should stay with those with virtues and humaneness and learn from them first if he is to be a humane person.

78. 工欲善其事，必先利其器

【原文】

子贡问为仁。子曰："工欲善其事，必先利其器。居是邦也，事其大夫之贤者，友其士之仁者。"

《论语·卫灵公》15.10 章

【释文】

子贡问怎样实行仁德。孔子说："做工的人想把活儿做好，必须首先使他的工具锋利。住在这个国家，就要事奉大夫中的那些贤者，与士人中的仁者交朋友。"

【解析】

孔子此处以"做工先磨刀"为喻，说明要想施行仁德，先要与贤能、仁德之人在一块，向他们学习。

人无远虑，必有近忧
He who lacks long-term plans will have worries at hand

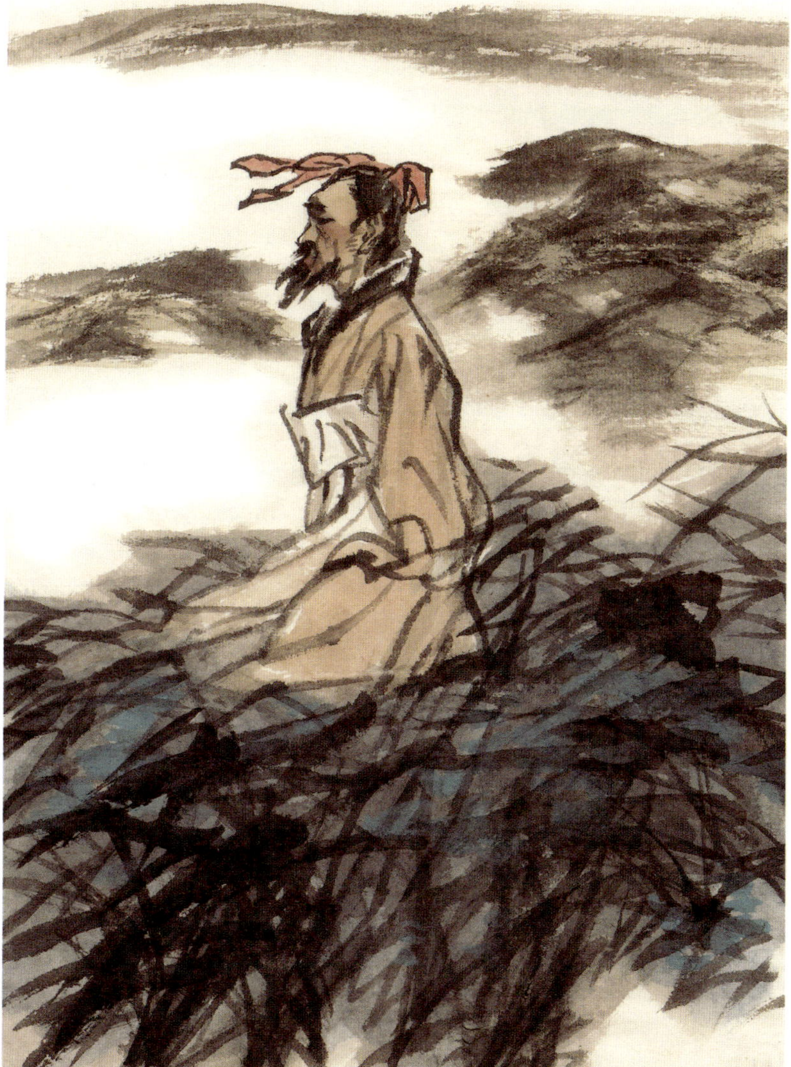

79. He who lacks long-term plans will have worries at hand

【Source】

The master said, "He who lacks long-term plans will have worries at hand."

The *Analects* ·Wei Ling Gong Chapter15.12

【Comments】

Men should have long-term plans and implement them step by step. Without long-term plans, men will be aimless, which will incur troubles.

79. 人无远虑，必有近忧

【原文】

子曰："人无远虑，必有近忧。"

《论语·卫灵公》15.12 章

【释文】

孔子说："人没有长远的考虑，一定会有眼前的忧患。"

【解析】

人有长远考虑，就会做好规划，从当前开始，一步步去实施；人无长远考虑，做事就漫无头绪、没有计划，以致面临不测而不知所措、遭致忧患。

80. Reproach others less and question yourself more

【Source】

The master said, "Reproaching others less and questioning yourself more will keep you away from others' resentment."

The *Analects* ·Wei Ling Gong Chapter15.15

【Comments】

A sound interpersonal relationship will be maintained if one is strict with himself and tolerant towards others.

80. 躬自厚而薄责于人

【原文】

子曰:"躬自厚而薄责于人,则远怨矣。"

《论语·卫灵公》15.15 章

【释文】

孔子说:"多责备自己而少责备别人,那就可以避免别人的怨恨了。"

【解析】

对待自己要严格,对待别人要宽容,这样才能保持良好和谐的人际关系。

81. Do not recommend a person because of his words. Do not ignore a person's good suggestions because of his deeds

【Source】

The master said, "The man of noble character will not recommend a person because of his words, nor will he ignore a person's good suggestions because of his deeds."

The *Analects* ·Wei Ling Gong Chapter15.23

【Comments】

Confucius analyzed the relations between a person's character and his words and deeds. He believed that a person should not be recommended because his words made him look like the man with virtues, nor should his words be ignored because of his character flaws.

81. 不以言举人，不以人废言

【原文】

子曰："君子不以言举人，不以人废言。"

《论语·卫灵公》15.23 章

【释文】

孔子说："君子不凭一个人说的话来举荐他，也不因为一个人不好而不采纳他的好话。"

【解析】

孔子这里分析人品与言论的关系，认为不能仅凭一个人的言论而认为他是贤人而举荐他，也不能因为一个人人品上的不足就一概否定其言论。

己所不欲，勿施于人
Do not impose on others what you yourself do not desire

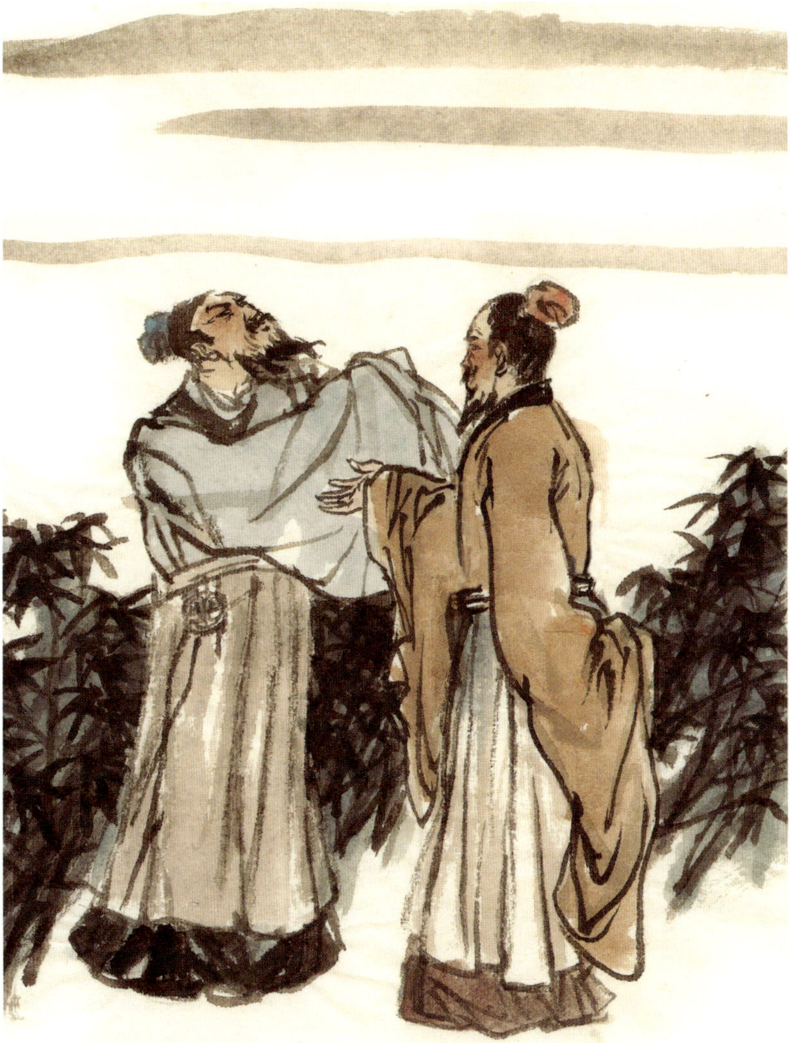

82. Do not impose on others what you yourself do not desire

【Source】

Zigong asked, "Is there one word that we can stick to in our whole life?"

The master said, "Reciprocity. Do not impose on others what you yourself do not desire."

The *Analects* ·Wei Ling Gong Chapter15.24

【Comments】

Reciprocity refers to treating others with humaneness, putting oneself into others' shoes and helping others fulfill their virtuous purposes. It's a Confucian principle of handling interpersonal relationship.

82. 己所不欲，勿施于人

【原文】

子贡问曰："有一言而可以终身行之者乎？"子曰："其恕乎！己所不欲，勿施于人。"

《论语·卫灵公》15.24 章

【释文】

子贡问："有没有一句话可以终身奉行呢？"孔子说："那就是恕吧！自己不愿意的，不要强加给别人。"

【解析】

"恕"就是以仁爱之心待人，替别人着想，能将心比心、推己及人、与人为善、成人之美，这是儒家处理人己关系的一条准则。

83. Lack of patience in small matters leads to the disruption of great plans

【Source】

The master said, "Clever words disrupt virtue. Lack of patience in small matters leads to the disruption of great plans."

The *Analects* ·Wei Ling Gong Chapter15.27

【Comments】

The saying that "lack of patience in small matters leads to the disruption of great plans" is popular and a lot of people take it as their motto. Men with noble ideas should be far-sighted and broad-minded.

83. 小不忍则乱大谋

【原文】

子曰:"巧言乱德,小不忍则乱大谋。"

《论语·卫灵公》15.27 章

【释文】

孔子说:"花言巧语败坏人的德行,小事情不忍耐就会败坏大事情。"

【解析】

"小不忍则乱大谋",这句话后世极为流行,成为许多人用以告诫自己的座右铭。有志向、有理想的人,应眼光远大、胸襟宽广,不应在眼前小事上纠缠不清、斤斤计较。

众恶之，必察焉
If one is hated by all, find out reasons

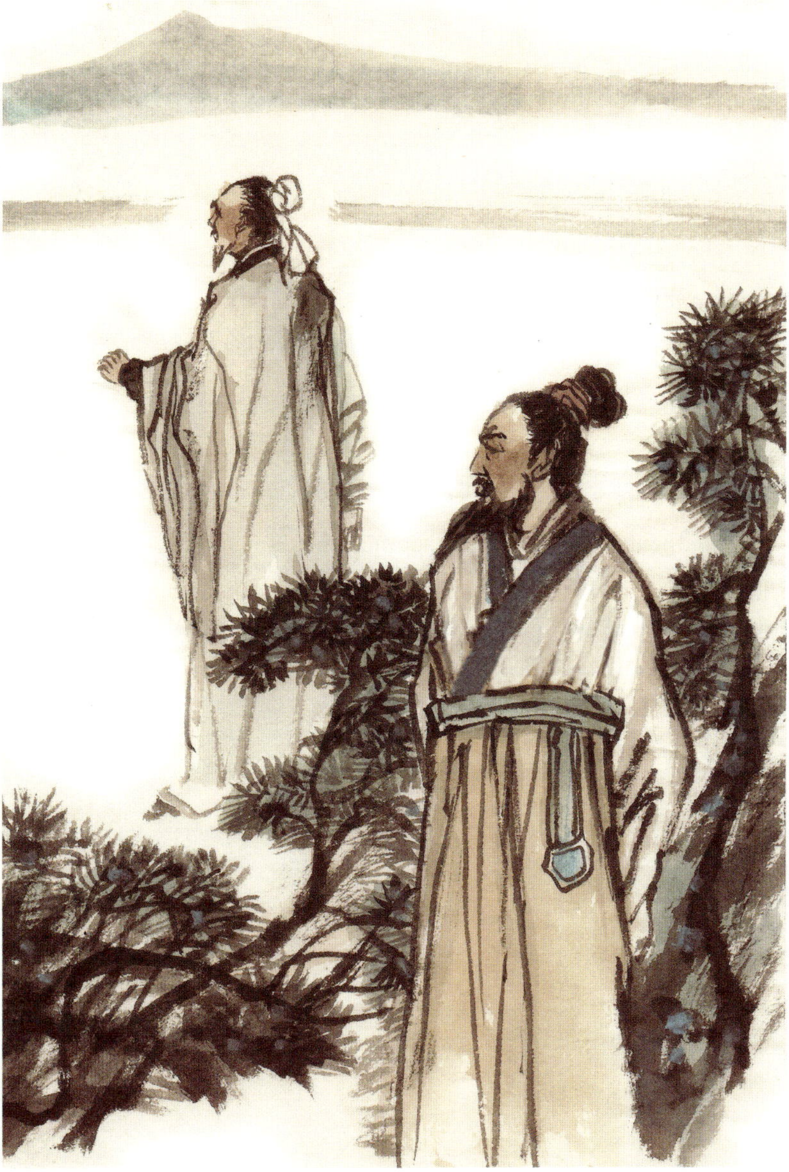

84.If one is hated by all, find out reasons

【Source】

The master said, "If one is hated by all, find out reasons. If one is loved by all, find out reasons."

The *Analects* ·Wei Ling Gong Chapter15.28

【Comments】

Confucius held the belief that men should not follow the herd and should have critical thinking and act on their own judgment.

84. 众恶之，必察焉

【原文】

子曰："众恶之，必察焉；众好之，必察焉。"

《论语·卫灵公》15.28 章

【释文】

孔子说："大家都厌恶他，一定要考察这是为什么；大家都喜欢他，一定要考察这是为什么。"

【解析】

孔子主张评价人不能人云亦云、随波逐流，对大家厌恶的人如此，对大家喜爱的人也应如此，都要经过自己的调查判断、独立思考。

85. It's men who carry forward the Way

【Source】

The master said, "It's men who carry forward the Way, not vice versa."

The Analects ·Wei Ling Gong Chapter15.29

【Comments】

Men can improve their self-cultivation and play a positive role in carrying forward the Way. If putting aside the Way without learning it, its role cannot be played. The man of noble character will not take the Way as window dressing or use it to enhance his standing.

85. 人能弘道

【原文】

子曰:"人能弘道,非道弘人。"

《论语·卫灵公》15.29 章

【释文】

孔子说:"人能够使道发扬光大,不是道使人的名声显扬。"

【解析】

人可以发挥能动作用,修养自身,把道发扬光大。反过来,把道放在一旁不去学习,并不能发挥道的作用。用道来装点门面,哗众取宠,抬高身价,更不是君子之所为。

过而不改，是谓过矣
A mistake is a real mistake if not corrected

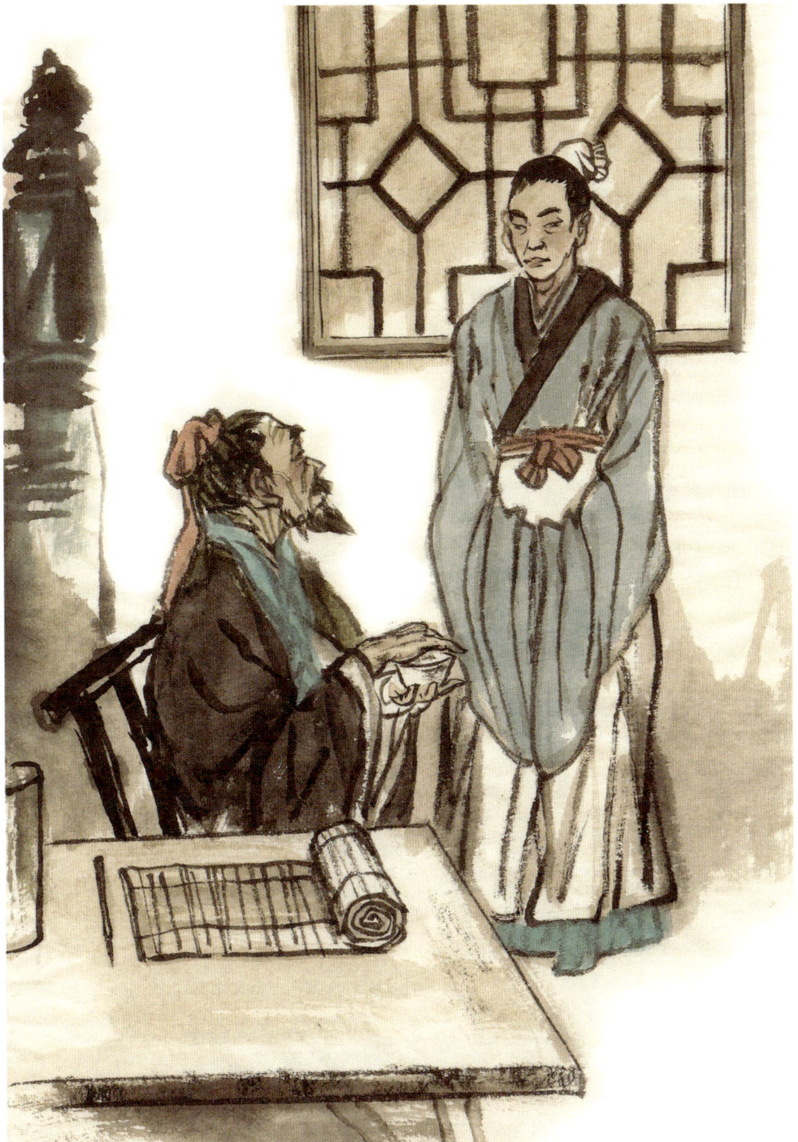

86. A mistake is a real mistake if not corrected

【Source】

The master said, "A mistake is a real mistake if not corrected."

The *Analects* ·Wei Ling Gong Chapter15.30

【Comments】

It's the nature of every one to make mistakes. It is not mistakes that are terrible, but persistence in mistakes and refusal to correct them. A wise person will correct his mistakes and make sure not to make the same one in the future.

86. 过而不改，是谓过矣

【原文】

子曰："过而不改，是谓过矣。"

《论语·卫灵公》15.30 章

【释文】

孔子说："有了过错而不改正，这才真叫过错。"

【解析】

人都会犯错误，有了过错并不可怕，可怕的是坚持错误，不加改正。优秀的人有了过错会积极改正，保证今后不再犯同样的错误。

87. Students don't have to be inferior to their teachers concerning humaneness

【Source】

The master said, "Students don't have to be inferior to their teachers concerning humaneness."

The Analects ·Wei Ling Gong Chapter15.36

【Comments】

Confucius attached great importance to the harmonious teacher-student relationship and emphasized respects for teachers. However, students don't have to be inferior to their teachers concerning humaneness as Confucius put humaneness first.

87. 当仁，不让于师

【原文】

子曰："当仁，不让于师。"

《论语·卫灵公》15.36 章

【释文】

孔子说："面对着仁德，就是老师，也不同他谦让。"

【解析】

孔子特别重视师生关系的和谐，强调师道尊严，但在仁德面前，学生却不必跟老师谦让，因为孔子把实现仁德摆在第一位。

有教无类

Teach all with no discrimination

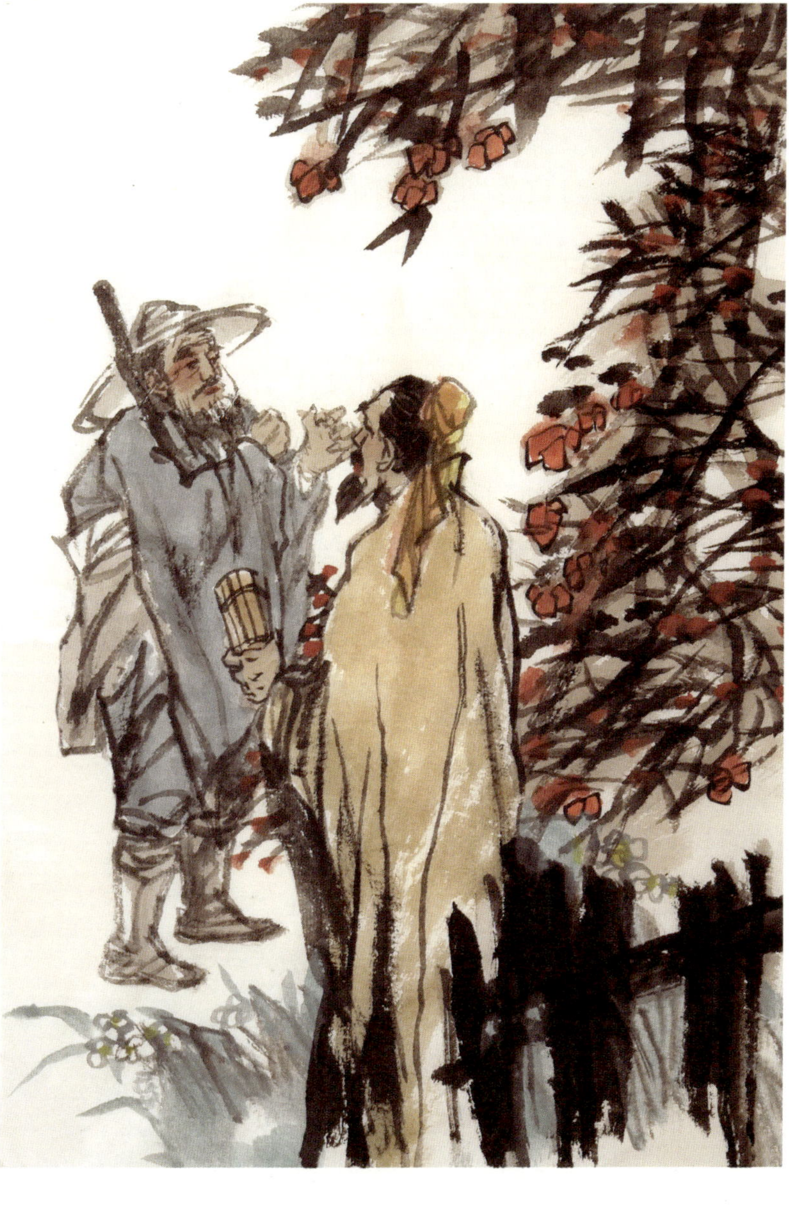

88. Teach all with no discrimination

【Source】

The master said, "I'd like to teach all with no discrimination."

The *Analects* ·Wei Ling Gong Chapter15.39

【Comments】

As a great educator in ancient China, Confucius held the belief that all young people regardless of their background should have access to education, so he broke the tradition of schools run by government to start private teaching and recruit as many disciples as he could.

88. 有教无类

【原文】

子曰:"有教无类。"

《论语·卫灵公》15.39 章

【释文】

孔子说:"人人我都可以教育,不因贫富贵贱而不同。"

【解析】

孔子是中国古代伟大的教育家,主张各阶层子弟都应有受教育的机会,因而开创私学,广招门徒,打破了学在官府的局面。

89. The trouble lies not in a small population but in uneven distribution of wealth, not in poverty but in instability

【Source】

The trouble lies not in a small population but in uneven distribution of wealth, not in poverty but in instability. When wealth is evenly distributed, poverty is out of question. When people live in harmony, a small population is out of question. When a country maintains stability, subversion is out of question. After realizing the above and if those living in remote areas still do not subject them to the ruler, win them over by means of humaneness, righteousness, rites and music. When they come, let them stay.

The Analects ·Ji Shi Chapter16.1

【Comments】

Confucius depicted an ideal society where wealth was evenly distributed. His idea exerts profound influence on future generations. Confucius was against invasion and war, but for harmony and benevolence. He believed that rulers should subject people living in remote areas to them by means of humaneness, righteousness, rites and music.

89. 不患寡而患不均，不患贫而患不安

【原文】

有国有家者，不患寡而患不均，不患贫而患不安。盖均无贫，和无寡，安无倾。夫如是，故远人不服，则修文德以来之；既来之，则安之。

《论语·季氏》16.1 章

【释文】

诸侯和大夫，不怕人口少而怕财富不均，不怕贫穷而怕不安定。这是因为财富平均了就没有所谓贫穷，大家和睦了就不会感到人少，国家安定了就没有倾覆的危险。要做到这样，则远方的人如果还不归服，就用仁、义、礼、乐招徕他们；已经招他们来了，就让他们安心住下去。

【解析】

孔子此处提出了财富平均的社会理想，对后世有重大影响。孔子反对侵略攻伐，主张用仁、义、礼、乐感化、吸引远方之人，以求亲善和睦。

90. The man of noble character should always guard against three things

【Source】

The master said, "The man of noble character should always guard against three things: when young and his body is still growing, he should guard against lust of young women; when at his prime of life, he should guard against fighting; when old, his body begins aging and he should guard against gains."

The Analects ·Ji Shi Chapter16.7

【Comments】

Confucius cautioned people to guard against three things when they were young, at their prime of life and old based on the law of body growth for the sake of a happy and comfortable life.

90. 君子有三戒

【原文】

孔子曰："君子有三戒：少之时，血气未定，戒之在色；及其壮也，血气方刚，戒之在斗；及其老也，血气既衰，戒之在得。"

《论语·季氏》16.7 章

【释文】

孔子说："君子有三种事情应引以为戒：年少的时候，血气还不成熟，要戒除对女色的迷恋；等到身体成熟了，血气方刚，要戒除与人争斗；到了老年，血气已经衰弱了，要戒除贪得无厌。"

【解析】

孔子这里根据人血气的成长、盛衰，对人从少年到壮年再到老年这一生中三大阶段须要注意的问题作出忠告，以求平和安稳。

性相近也，习相远也
By nature, men are much alike; but in practice, they are far apart

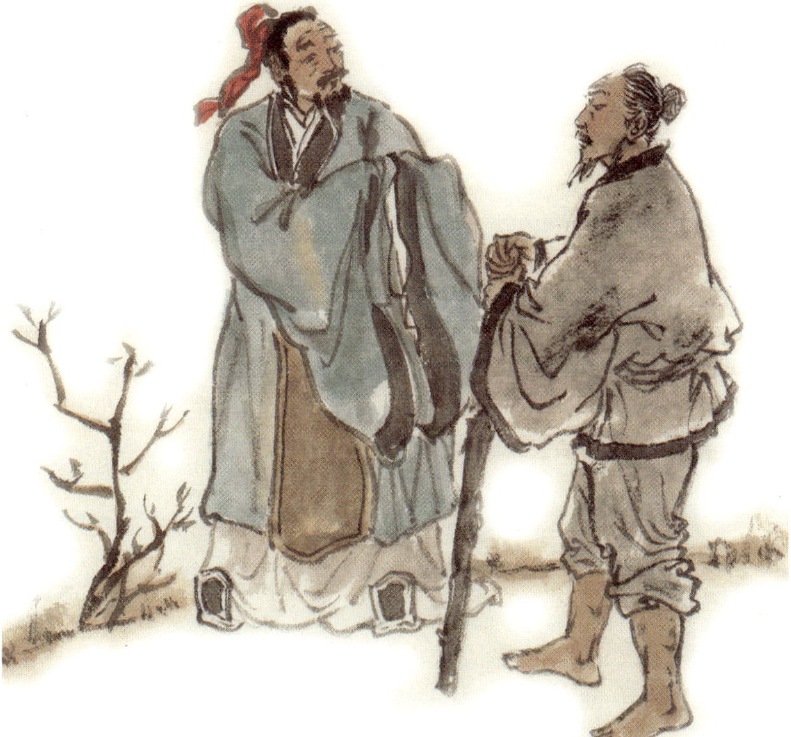

91. By nature, men are much alike; but in practice, they are far apart

【Source】

The master said, "By nature, men are much alike; but in practice, they are far apart."

The *Analects* ·Yang Huo Chapter17.2

【Comments】

Confucius believed that men had similar nature, but became different due to learning and environment. Men should pay more attention to influence of learning and their surroundings on them.

91. 性相近也，习相远也

【原文】

子曰："性相近也，习相远也。"

《论语·阳货》17.2 章

【释文】

孔子说："人性情本相近，因为习染不同，便相距很远了。"

【解析】

孔子认为人的先天本性是差不多的，但由于后天个人的学习和环境的影响便拉开了差距，区分了善恶。因此，人应当更加重视自身的学习以及周围环境对自己的影响。

92. He who likes humaneness but dislikes learning will be fooled

【Source】

The master said, "You, have you heard of six virtues and their corresponding drawbacks?" Ziyou answered, "No." The master said, "Sit by my side and let me tell you. He who likes humaneness but dislikes learning will be fooled. He who likes wisdom but dislikes learning will have superficial knowledge. He who likes integrity but dislikes learning will be credulous and easy to get hurt. He who likes straightforwardness but dislikes learning will be sharp-tongued and hurt others. He who likes bravery but dislikes learning will behave impulsively and cause trouble. He who likes staunchness but dislikes learning will be aggressive and reckless."

The *Analects* ·Yang Huo Chapter 17.8

【Comments】

Virtues will be transformed into drawbacks if one dislikes learning and lacks a correct understanding. Learning is the basis of moral cultivation and moral levels will be increased through continuous learning.

92. 好仁不好学，其蔽也愚

【原文】

子曰："由也，女闻六言六蔽矣乎？"对曰："未也。""居！吾语女。好仁不好学，其蔽也愚；好知不好学，其蔽也荡；好信不好学，其蔽也贼；好直不好学，共蔽也绞；好勇不好学，其蔽也乱；好刚不好学，其蔽也狂。"

《论语·阳货》17.8 章

【释文】

孔子说："仲由啊，你听说过用六个字来概括的六种品德和可能产生的六种弊病吗？"子路回答说："没有。"孔子说："坐下，我告诉你吧。喜好'仁'却不喜好学，其弊病是容易受人愚弄；喜好'智'却不喜好学，其弊病是学问浮荡无根；喜好'信'却不喜好学，其弊病是易轻信而受伤害；喜好'直'却不喜好学，其弊病是说话急切尖刻容易伤人；喜好'勇'却不喜好学，其弊病是逞勇斗狠作乱闯祸；喜好'刚'却不喜好学，其弊病是争强好胜胆大妄为。"

【解析】

不好学，缺乏正确的认识，美德也会变质，"六德"变成"六弊"，走向它的反面。可见，好学是修德的基础，只有不断学习，才能不断完善德行。

93. How can he with a full stomach but empty head achieve something?

【Source】

The master said, "How can he with a full stomach but empty head achieve something? Better spending time in playing games than remaining idle."

The *Analects* ·Yang Huo Chapter 17.22

【Comments】

Confucius criticized people for idling their time away.

93. 饱食终日，无所用心，难矣哉

【原文】

子曰："饱食终日，无所用心，难矣哉！不有博弈者乎？为之，犹贤乎已。"

《论语·阳货》17.22 章

【释文】

孔子说："整天吃饱了饭，任何用心尽力的事都不做，这种人难有长进啊！不是有掷采、下棋的游戏吗？做这些事也比闲着好。"

【解析】

孔子批评那种不动心思、浑浑噩噩的精神状态。

往者不可谏，来者犹可追
The past cannot be retrieved, yet the future can be remedied

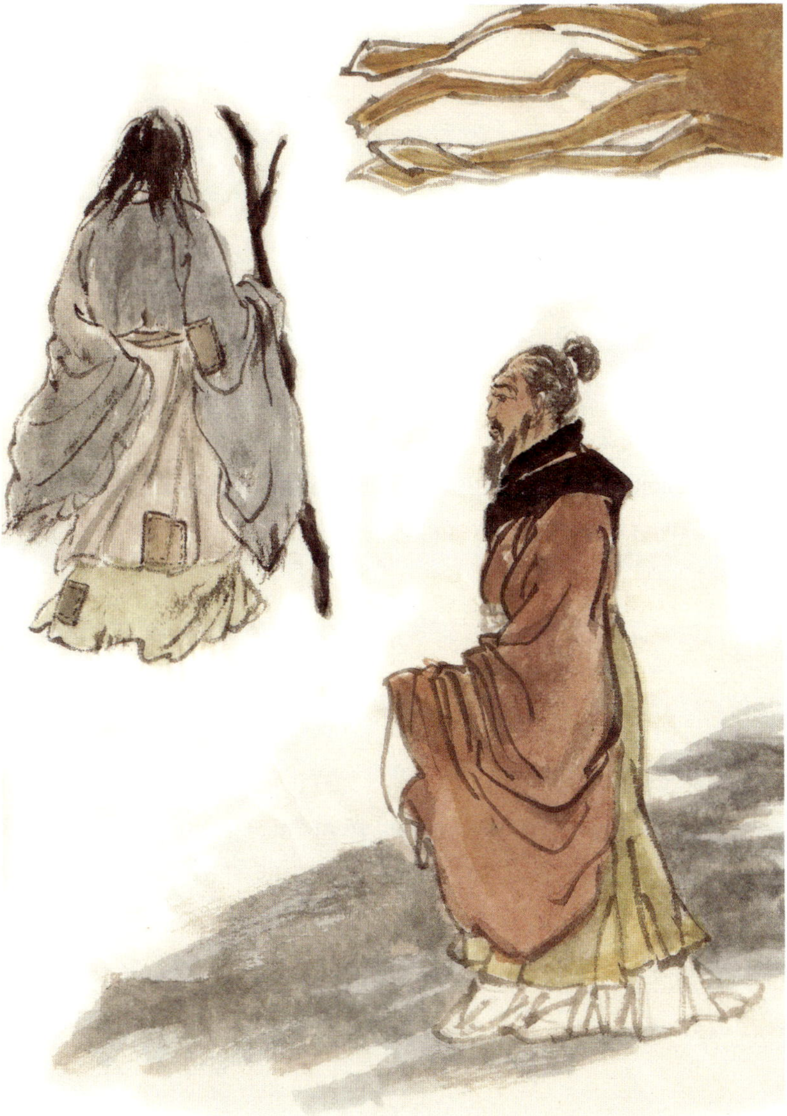

94. The past cannot be retrieved, yet the future can be remedied

【Source】

Jieyu, an unrestrained man from the State of Chu sung when passing by the carriage of Confucius, "Phoenix, phoenix, how come your morals are declined? The past cannot be retrieved, yet the future can be remedied. Let it go. Let it go. It's quite a danger to be an official at this moment."

Confucius went out of his carriage and wanted to approach Jieyu, but he walked away instantly and Confucius could not have a chance to talk with him.

The *Analects* ·Weizi Chapter18.5

【Comments】

Jieyu was an unrestrained hermit from the State of Chu. He likened Confucius to phoenix and thought that Confucius should resign and live in seclusion as he could accomplish nothing in troubled times. Confucius wanted to talk with Jieyu after listening to what he said, but in vain.

94. 往者不可谏，来者犹可追

【原文】

楚狂接舆歌而过孔子曰："凤兮凤兮！何德之衰？往者不可谏，来者犹可追。已而，已而！今之从政者殆而！"孔子下，欲与之言。趋而辟之，不得与之言。

《论语·微子》18.5 章

【释文】

楚国的狂人接舆走过孔子的车子时唱道："凤凰啊，凤凰啊！你的品德为什么这样衰败呢？过去的不能再挽回，未来的还可补救。算了吧，算了吧！现今从政的人危险极了！"孔子下车，想同他谈谈，他却赶快避开，孔子没能同他交谈。

【解析】

接舆是楚国的一个隐士，性情狂傲，他把孔子比喻为凤鸟，认为孔子生逢乱世不可能有所作为，不如归隐。孔子听后想与他交流而未能实现。

士见危致命，见得思义
Scholars sacrifice their lives in times of danger,
keep righteousness in mind in front of profits

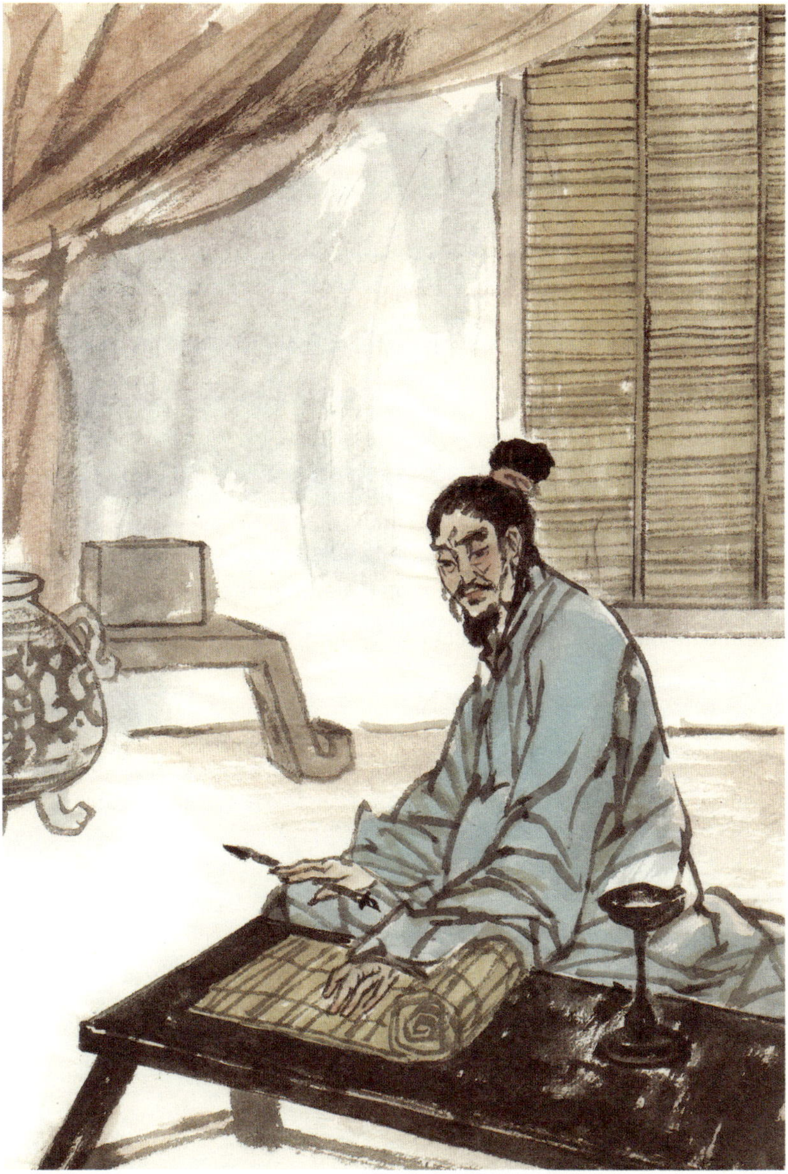

95. Scholars sacrifice their lives in times of danger, keep righteousness in mind in front of profits

【Source】

Zizhang said, "Scholars who sacrifice their lives in times of danger, keep righteousness in mind in front of profits, behave reverently at sacrificial ceremonies and feel mournful at funerals are scholars indeed."

The *Analects* ·Zizhang Chapter19.1

【Comments】

Zizhang pointed out basic moral requirements for scholars. Inner moral cultivation has its external expressions.

95. 士见危致命，见得思义

【原文】

子张曰："士见危致命，见得思义，祭思敬，丧思哀，其可已矣。"

《论语·子张》19.1 章

【释文】

子张说："读书人看见危险肯豁出生命来担当，看见有所得便考虑是否该得，祭祀时严肃恭敬，居丧时悲痛哀伤，那也就可以了。"

【解析】

子张提出读书人德行的基本要求，内在的德行要有外在的表现。

96. Learn extensively while sticking to one's interests, ask questions earnestly and give more thoughts to the current issues

【Source】

Zixia said, "Learn extensively while sticking to one's interests, ask questions earnestly and give more thoughts to the current issues. By doing so, humaneness is shown."

The Analects ·Zizhang Chapter19.6

【Comments】

Zixia pointed out that humaneness was cultivated through learning extensively while sticking to one's interests, asking questions earnestly and giving more thoughts to the current issues.

96. 博学笃志，切问近思

【原文】

子夏曰："博学而笃志，切问而近思，仁在其中矣。"

《论语·子张》19.6 章

【释文】

子夏说："广泛地学习，坚守自己的志趣；恳切地发问，多考虑当前的问题，仁德就在这中间了。"

【解析】

子夏提出修养仁德的方法，即博学多问，坚守志趣，关注现实。

学而优则仕

A scholar, after completing his learning,
should devote himself to duties as an official

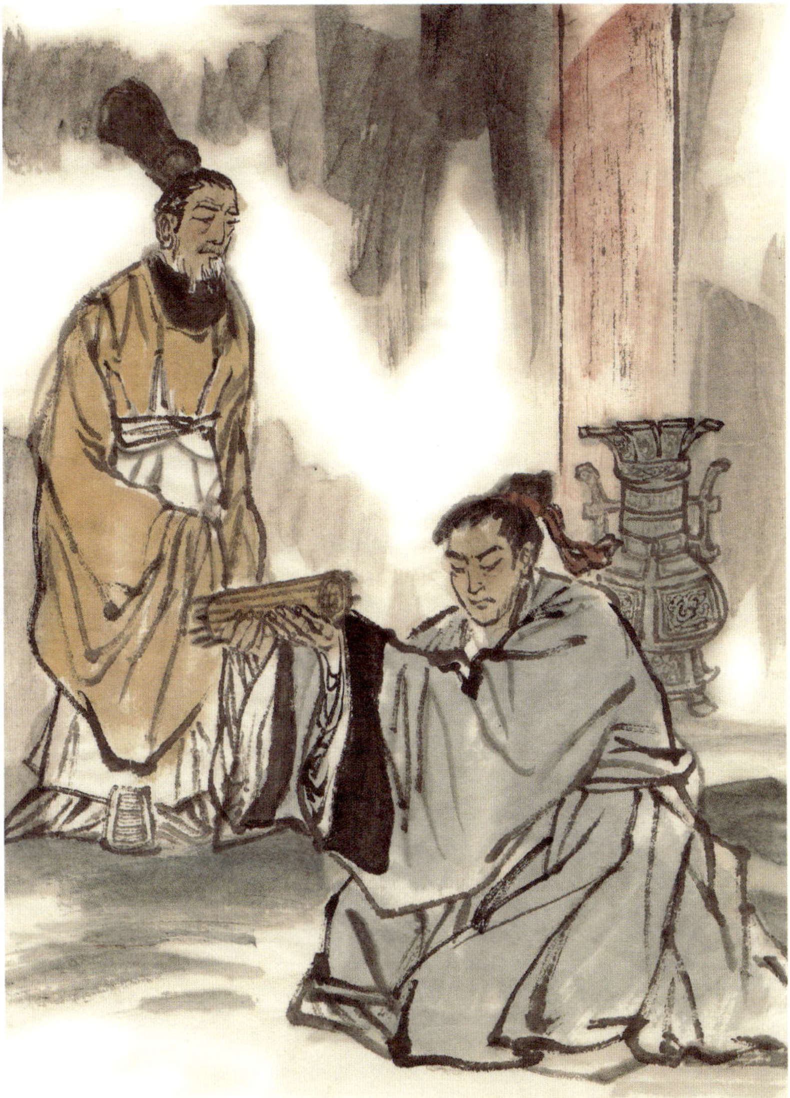

97. A scholar, after completing his learning, should devote himself to duties as an official

【Source】

Zixia said, "An official, after performing his duties, should devote himself to learning. A scholar, after completing his learning, should devote himself to duties as an official."

The Analects ·Zizhang Chapter19.13

【Comments】

The chapter reveals the relations and the interplay between officialdom and learning. It stresses the importance of continuous learning to both officials and scholars.

97. 学而优则仕

【原文】

子夏曰:"仕而优则学,学而优则仕。"

《论语·子张》19.13 章

【释文】

子夏说:"做官有余力便可去学习,学习有余力便可去做官。"

【解析】

本章揭示了做官与求学的关系,要求无论做官还是求学,都应当以学习为重,不断地充实自己。同时也表明,学与仕结合,方能相互促进,相得益彰。

君子之过也，如日月之食焉

Mistakes made by the man of noble character
are like eclipses of the sun and the moon

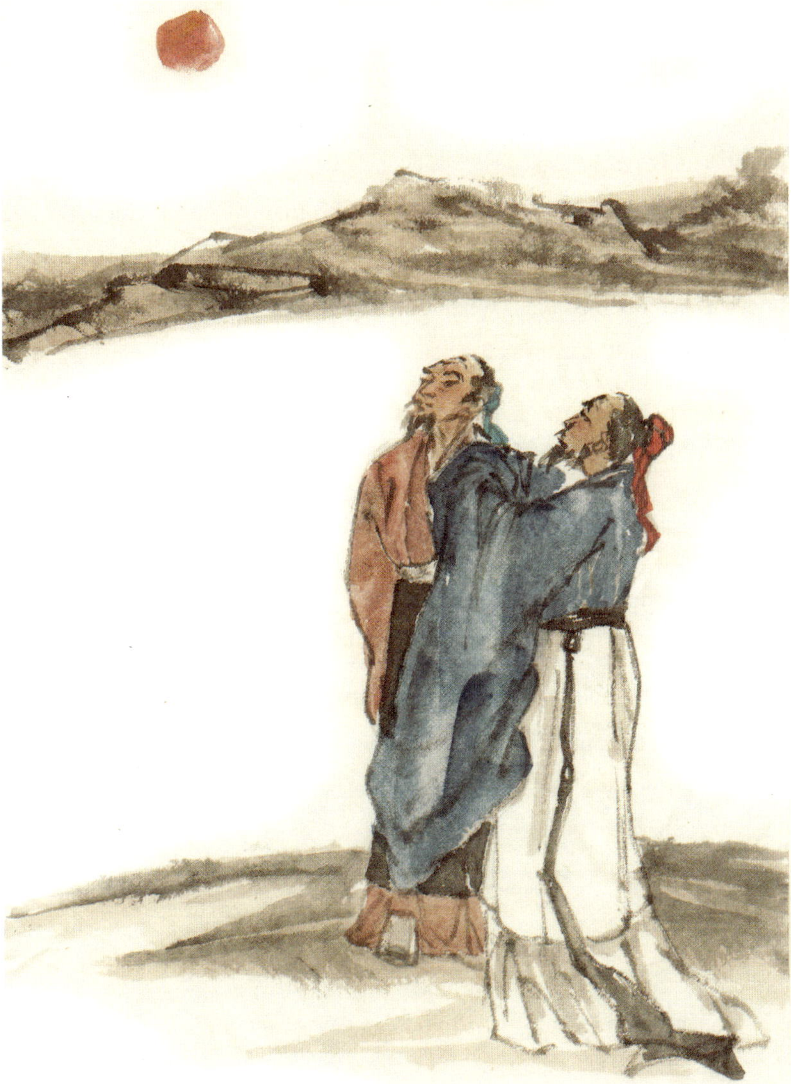

98.Mistakes made by the man of noble character are like eclipses of the sun and the moon

【Source】

Zigong said, "Mistakes made by the man of noble character are like eclipses of the sun and the moon. When he makes mistakes, every one will see his mistakes. When he corrects his mistakes, every one will look up to him."

The *Analects* ·Zizhang Chapter19.21

【Comments】

The chapter likens mistakes made by the man of noble character to eclipses of the sun and the moon. When he makes a mistake, he will be seen by the public and when he corrects his mistakes, he will earn respect from the public.

98. 君子之过也，如日月之食焉

【原文】

子贡曰："君子之过也，如日月之食焉：过也，人皆见之；更也，人皆仰之。"

《论语·子张》19.21 章

【释文】

子贡说："君子的过失好比日食和月食：他犯错的时候，每个人都看得见；他改过的时候，每个人都仰望着他。"

【解析】

本章用日食和月食比喻君子的过失，他犯错时容易被大众看到，知错能改则能得到大众的尊敬。

99.Direct people to get what are beneficial to them

【Source】

The master said, "Direct people to get what are beneficial to them."

The *Analects* ·Yao Yue Chapter20.2

【Comments】

Politicians should respect opinions of the public and bring benefits to common people.

99. 因民之所利而利之

【原文】

子曰:"因民之所利而利之。"

《论语·尧曰》20.2章

【释文】

孔子说:"看人民在哪些方面能得利,就引导他们去得利。"

【解析】

尊重民意,适当引导,给民众以实惠,这是为政者应该做的事。

100. He who doesn't know his destiny will not be the man of noble character

【Source】

The master said, "He who doesn't know his destiny will not be the man of noble character. He who doesn's know the rites will not be established in the society. He who cannot distinguish right and wrong in others' words will not know people."

The *Analects* ·Yao Yue Chapter20.3

【Comments】

The chapter discusses how to acquit oneself well, how to be established in the society and how to deal with others. One will have no worries about results and find it easy to accept what his life brings to him, weather it is good or bad when knowing his destiny. One will behave in a proper way and be established in the society when knowing the rites. Communication is the most important way in associating with others. One can understand others' thoughts through their words, which will help him to associate with them.

100. 不知命，无以为君子也

【原文】

孔子曰："不知命，无以为君子也；不知礼，无以立也；不知言，无以知人也。"

《论语·尧曰》20.3 章

【释文】

孔子说："不懂得天命，没有可能成为君子；不懂得礼，没有可能立足于社会；不懂得分辨他人的言语，没有可能认识人。"

【解析】

本章谈的是人如何自处、自立和与人相处。懂得天命，就不再为结果烦恼，坦然面对人生。懂得礼，行为就符合天道，也就能立于天地之间，站稳脚跟。人与人交往最重要的是说话，通过言语，可以辨别人的思想、情操、境界，从容地与他人交往。